SIMPLY RED AND GREEN

Simply Red and Green

MANCHESTER UNITED AND IRELAND:
A STORY OF A LOVE AFFAIR

JOHN SCALLY

Foreword by Bertie Ahern

EDINBURGH AND LONDON

First published in Great Britain in 1998 by
MAINSTREAM PUBLISHING COMPANY (EDINBURGH) LTD
7 Albany Street
Edinburgh EH1 3UG

ISBN 1 84018 048 X

A catalogue record for this book is available from the British Library

Typeset in Book Antiqua
Printed and bound in Great Britain by Butler and Tanner Ltd, Frome

To the memory of Veronica Guerin:

... a mind
that nobleness made simple like a fire.
With beauty like a tightened bow, a kind,
that is not natural in an age like this.

Contents

Acknowledgements

Thanks to Terry Behan, Paddy Joe Burke, Jack Charlton, Ken Doherty, Connell Dorris, Gavin Duffy, Eamon Dunphy, Dermot Earley, Gerry Francis, Billy Gibbons, Eddie Gibbons, John Giles, Barry Kehoe, Alan Kerneghan, Paul McGrath, Manchester United Supporters Club Ireland, Noel Mannion, Frank Mullen, Ronnie Nolan, Nick Ready, Ray Treacy, Gary Waddock and Christy Whelan.

As always, I am grateful to my good friend Noel Coughlan for his practical assistance.

With great sadness I acknowledge my debt to the late, great Dermot Morgan – who died during the writing of this book – for permission to use material from *Scrap Saturday*.

I am indebted to all at Mainstream Publishing, especially John Beaton, Andrew Laycock, Cathy Mineards and, in particular, Bill Campbell.

Very special thanks to Graham Turley, to Cathal Turley for modelling for the back cover and to an Taoiseach, Bertie Ahern TD.

Foreword
by an Taoiseach, Bertie Ahern TD

Football has a unique ability to nurture loyalties that in the main tend to last a lifetime, an appeal no doubt the envy of many practitioners of my own profession. It is a loyalty developed perhaps at a stage when a team is enjoying good fortune, and sustained during those inevitable barren periods where success can often be a distant memory. Even the departure of idols to pastures new cannot diminish the association with a chosen club. My club is Manchester United.

I belong to a generation of supporters whose earliest recollection of this great football club is the most tragic event in its illustrious history. I was six years old at the time of the crash, and while the enormity of the carnage on that icebound runway at Munich was not fully appreciated by one so young, I clearly remember my soccer-mad older brothers waiting in anxious anticipation for news of their heroes. Perhaps it was the confirmation that Liam Whelan, a gifted 22-year-old from Cabra on my native northside Dublin, was among the dead that brought the full impact of the tragedy home. The wave of sympathy that followed served in no small measure to make Manchester United, in the years that followed the tragedy, the most popular club on this island and, arguably, throughout the world. It was a popularity, however, not based solely on emotion but on a new and exciting style of football that developed out of the rebuilding process which produced the Busby Babes. I had become a fan. Over 40 years later, I remain committed to my boyhood choice.

Much is made today of the influence brought to bear on British football by its legions of continental players, an influence which, I would argue, has been to its betterment. I would also argue that players from these shores have had a huge impact, particularly at Manchester United, such as Johnny Carey, their great post-war captain, Dunne and Brennan, inspirational in that glorious European team of '68, and Roy Keane, who for many is the club's greatest asset. And George Best, who to this day, many years after his playing career, continues to be the subject of one of the great football debates – was he the greatest player of all time? And what about Giles, Stapleton, Whiteside, Moran and McGrath, and many more? There have been too many to acknowledge individually in this foreword, but they are all legends.

Football is essentially a simple game only complicated by the science of analysis. For me it continues to be a source of tremendous enjoyment. Irrespective of their future fortunes, my favourite club will always be Manchester United.

Introduction

The importance of soccer in the Irish psyche is revealed in Gerry Conlon's telling observation after he was finally released from his grossly unjust incarceration in prison for the Guildford bombing: 'I felt as if I had scored a goal in the World Cup for Ireland.'

Manchester United have excited Irish soccer fans like no other team. Jeremy Novick in his much acclaimed *In a League of Their Own: The Maverick Managers* (Mainstream), claims that Old Trafford was 'the footballing home of glamour, of romance, of love'. He perceptively observes that as the '60s gave way to the '70s and the media's influence increased, various clubs' images gained popular currency. 'Leeds were Lee Van Cleef, all dark hats and snidey shots in the back; Liverpool were Clint Eastwood, quietly getting on with the business of coming out on top; Arsenal were something else, but something too dull to remember; Spurs were flash new cash; and Manchester United were aristocrats, not actually winning anything, but superior through breeding.'

He goes on to argue that, more than any other team, United was the club that 'traded in love'. Since the Munich disaster, Matt Busby and his babes, Best, Law *et al.*, 'the word United was soccer shorthand for romance'.

The world is fickle, but the footballing world will never forget what happened in 1958. The outpouring of sorrow and remembrance at the Munich disaster transcended anything in sporting history. The scars of such tragedy were not easily healed.

The United players lived lives of classic dimensions. As in war, so in tragedy. Cold logic is a casualty, albeit for different reasons. Powerful emotion reigns supreme and those who are bereaved cannot bear their entranced vision of what went before to be doubted or disturbed. Like a macabre twist in a soap opera the Munich crash elevated the players who died to icon status where they hover celestially over other lesser teams designed to navigate the collective psyche of football fans for decades to come. The accidental conjunction of talent, youth, public mood and historical event ensures their stars will never be extinguished.

Their funerals were like no other. Most funerals are a burial of something or someone already gone. The United players' young deaths pointed in exactly the opposite direction and were therefore all the more poignant. Normally we bury the past, but in burying Liam Whelan and his colleagues, in some deep and gnawing way we buried the future.

Memory is blurred and softened by time, so no other team can hope to emulate the mass appeal and hypnotic magnetism of the Busby babes. They could not do it in life and it would be even more difficult now that they are ageless in premature death. No other combination of players could possibly fill the void in the lives of those fans who now find themselves worshipping at United's shrine. Future United teams are now inextricably linked with their lives and deaths, an outcome nobody could have foreseen at the time.

Only a man for whom duty is second nature could have picked up the pieces after Munich. It is in moments of crisis that the true depths of character show, and Matt Busby's constitution was conclusively shown to be made of the right stuff. A lesser man would have been trapped in a numb emptiness which would generate crippling depression.

Of course, Busby was an Irishman – at least more so than many of the players who have lined out for the boys in green in recent decades. He was born in the Lanarkshire mining village of Orbiston in 1909. His maternal grandfather, Jimmy Greer, emigrated to Scotland from Ireland to find work in the pits. Busby's new team were a breath of fresh, evolved air in an era that reeked of pulsating excitement. They fitted the spirit of the '60s perfectly.

On a global basis the Mexico World Cup in 1970 elevated football to a new plane thanks to the miracle of television. While television had always been played and watched on a worldwide basis, the notion of football as an aesthetic pleasure did not become fashionable until the glories of Pele and Brazil's wonder team became evident to a mass audience. Up to then, television had been an optional extra rather than a constituent part of football education in a fundamentally formative sense.

The result was a new level of cultural power transmitted with unprecedented ferocity by the global media which shaped the mass consciousness almost subliminally. Many of us saw images of Manchester United players more frequently than we saw our parents or our siblings. As media staples they penetrated our lives more fully than many of our friends. This is mass-market culture, also exemplified today in Oasis, McDonald's, the internet and trips to Disneyland.

In the 1989 film *Field of Dreams* starring Kevin Costner, a farmer heard the corn telling him to build a baseball field at the back of his house. To many Irish fans Old Trafford has the same sense of mystery and religious calling. What is particularly remarkable about this obsession is that in a country where ecumenism has been so absent, this passion is shared by northern Protestants and southern Catholics alike.

The explanation for this mystique and fantasy goes much deeper than might appear on the surface. This is a story within a story – and as much a social history as a sports book.

Chapter One

Glory

---

*'Most of the things I've done are my own fault, so I can't feel
guilty about them.'*

— GEORGE BEST

Sport is agony and ecstasy; feast and famine. It does not lend itself
to grey areas. Sport is also about minute measurements – the gap
between glory and anguish. No one has learnt this lesson more
painfully than George Best. The difference between Best and the
rest is the difference between Pavarotti and Jason Donovan.

The late Danny Blanchflower remarked: 'Football is not about
winning, it's about glory.' Best's life has been a peculiar combination of glory and ignominy. His finest hour was at Wembley
the night Manchester United beat Benfica in 1968 to win the
European Cup final.

United went into the final with a considerable disadvantage.
They were denied the presence of Denis Law because of a knee
injury. The Best, Law and Charlton era represents the high-water
mark of post-war British football. No other team has had three
players named as European Footballer of the Year within the space
of five seasons. Law was the first of the three to win this accolade.

It was fitting that United's greatest glory should come exactly ten
years after the Munich disaster. On three occasions United had got
to the semi-finals of the European Cup only to fail the penultimate
test each time.

United's march to the final had taken them first to Malta, then to

Sarajevo, and finally to Poland – in a match that was played in horrendous conditions with two feet of snow on the pitch and temperatures of minus six degrees Celsius. In contrast their next fixture in Madrid was played at 90 degrees Fahrenheit. United had won 1–0 in the first leg at Old Trafford, though they found themselves 3–1 down at half-time in the second leg. After Matt Busby's pep talk at the interval, United squared the tie at 3–3.

The final, against the Portuguese side Benfica, was played at Wembley on the same day as Sir Ivor won the Derby. On any other day this race would have been the big sporting story, because there were so many fascinating ingredients. Mrs Alice Chandler was a descendant of the famous hunter Daniel Boone. She was also the woman who bred Sir Ivor. His owner Raymond Guest had won the Derby with Larkspur under the tutelage of Vincent O'Brien. Not surprisingly, Sir Ivor was sent to Ballydoyle also. After his first success his owner struck a £500 bet each way at 100–1 for the Derby with William Hill. The bet received almost as much publicity as the horse's rapidly ascending career. In 1968 Lester Piggott faced a dilemma: whether to ride Sir Ivor or the unbeaten Petingo, trained by his father-in-law, Sam Armstrong. Piggott's decision to opt for Sir Ivor was vindicated when he won by one and a half lengths. Although the horse had established his speed and mile-and-a-quarter pedigree, the experts claimed Sir Ivor was unlikely to stay the distance in the Derby. The O'Brien–Piggott partnership thought otherwise and came up with a masterplan. Sir Ivor stayed with the bunch until the last possible moment, when Piggott switched and thrust for the line, beating Connaught by one and a half lengths, having hit the front less than 50 yards from the line.

However, the following morning it was United who were splashed all over the front pages. The result provoked astonishing celebrations – a kind of footballing catharsis, an outpouring of affection built up over ten years for a team which had suffered so much.

To get free from the hype on the day of the final the Red Devils went to Surrey, where misfortune struck Brian Kidd when he fell into a pond and found himself literally up to his neck in mud. All the team, regardless of religious denomination, went to a special Mass organised in a local Catholic school.

On a scorching hot night the United team got a boost when they approached the ground. Although there were thousands of fans outside, what impressed them most was a group of 30 Egyptians who stood with a banner: *Manchester United Supporters Club Cairo Branch.*

United wore blue on the night because Benfica also played in red. The half-time score was 0–0, but in the second half Bobby Charlton scored with a header which went in at the foot of the post. United then made a near-fatal mistake by trying to hold on to possession. The Portuguese equalised late in the game and the legendary Eusebio was then clean through in the dying moments, but Alex Stepney made a brilliant save. The match went to extra-time.

It was fitting that it was Best who broke the deadlock when he dribbled around the goalie, having slipped the ball through the centre-half's legs. The team relaxed and a Brian Kidd goal followed by a great Bobby Charlton second goal sealed United's victory.

It was Best, though, who stole the show with his unique marriage of the graceful and dramatic. Few players had the power to affect a crowd's response as much as he did. Every time he got the ball something extraordinary was expected of him. The crowd held its breath in expectation. More often than not they were not disappointed. 1968 was Best's year. Never one to miss out on the headlines, he was voted both English and European Footballer of the Year and topped the First Division scoring charts with 28 goals.

Within a few seasons he had become a cult figure, a living James Dean – but a rebel *with* a cause. More accurately, he had two causes: to help Matt Busby achieve his lifetime ambition to make Manchester United the kings of Europe, and, more personally, to establish himself as the greatest player of all time. He was a riddle wrapped in an enigma: the creator of a new glamorous image for football, while simultaneously turning back the clock to an almost forgotten era of individuality in an age of the tyranny of convention. A creature of instinct rather than logic, his party trick was to drop a penny piece on the toe of his shoe, then flick it up into his top breast pocket. He was the stuff of magic.

He was the first footballing icon in the global village and one of its greatest ever celebrities – and celebrity is perhaps the most potent form of contemporary magic. United's European Cup win was the triumph of magic.

Best's was an incredible story. It started out as the supreme *Roy of the Rovers* story. But then, as the fairy tale turned to soap opera, he became something more, a kind of one-man rainbow coalition of every imaginable trauma from imprisonment to marriage breakdown, from public humiliation to global adulation. People have evoked fictional forms to express this – soap opera, morality play, Greek tragedy and, most often, fairy tale gone sour. The truth is that he was all of these and many more. Global communications have made his story more vivid than almost any we have ever known. But the essential appeal is ancient. It almost certainly predates written history. It is the appeal of the hero – albeit a slightly flawed hero.

In the autumn of his life Matt Busby said: 'George Best was probably the greatest player on the ball I have ever seen. You can remember Matthews, Finney and all the great players of the era, but I cannot think of one who took the ball so close to an opponent to beat him with it as Best did.'

Apart from Best, the United side that won the European Cup also featured two Republic of Ireland internationals: Shay Brennan and Tony Dunne (whom Bobby Charlton described as the best left-back in the world at the time). It was fitting, given the mutual love affair between Ireland and Manchester United, that this triumvirate would ensure that Ireland had a direct involvement in the most glorious chapter in United's history. The roots of this romance go very deep.

Chapter Two

The Dawning of
the Diaspora

This land, where every woman's son
Must carry his own coffin and believe,
In dread, all that the clergy teach the young.

— AUSTIN CLARKE

The Ireland of the 1840s was a vision of hell. They were the years of a tragedy beyond belief when over a million people on the tiny island died from famine. Nothing prepared people for it. Nothing could prepare anyone for the sight and smell of death on a massive scale, bundles of corpses where once there had been life.

The mid 1840s saw the plagues of Ireland – hunger, disease and government neglect. Each plague compounded the other like a battleground of contending dooms. Fragile lifelines of aid reached only a minority of the population. In the first year there were barely enough potatoes, in the next only a trickle. Then nothing. Potato stalks withered and died. There was nothing for seed. Many people had nothing to live on and nothing to live for.

The death toll was seemingly unending in many districts. Everything had to be rationed. It would have taken too much land to bury the corpses individually, so their relatives normally buried them in a mass grave. There were so many people dying it was impossible to make coffins for them all, or even have a coffin for each family. Timber was very scarce. Sometimes villagers decided to build one proper coffin with a sliding bottom. They solemnly put a corpse into the coffin, carried it up to the grave and slid back the bottom of the coffin to allow the body to tumble into the grave. The coffin was then brought back to the village and passed on to the family of the next casualty.

Fear was the only real sign of life as people died slowly, in agony. To the embattled, emotionally bankrupt and hopelessly disorganised, the ordinary joys and sorrows were an irrelevance. The chances of survival were slim. For many, death was a welcome escape from pain and heartache. The afterlife was the only dream they could still cherish. For the strong, life was a victory over death.

Where possible the corpses were buried under hawthorn trees because of their alleged special favour in the eyes of God. These trees were long palls in a parched place. They sang a lament to the angel of death. The memories were too sad ever to be forgotten.

Ireland was a country of extremes, from the beginning to the end. It seemed simultaneously connected to the Garden of Eden in the landlords' palaces and to some foretaste of doomsday destruction where the peasants lived to die. Nowhere were the gardens more luxuriant or a people more miserable. The tragedy was a moral test which those with power failed. There was plenty of food produced in Ireland during those years. That food was exported while Irish people starved in the country's greatest human tragedy is an enduring monument to inhumanity, ineffectiveness and indifference.

Stereotypes have done a great disservice to Irish history, and none more so than that which depicts Ireland as a priest-run society. The clergy have never had it all their own way in Ireland. Towards the end of the eighteenth century, for example, a bishop in the West of Ireland was afraid to disclose the fact that Rome had suppressed a number of festivals in honour of Our Lady, lest the news should provoke a riot. The Irish have always been delighted to follow their clergy – provided they are leading where the Irish want to go!

The most famous stereotype, though, is that of the avaricious, tyrannical English landlords. While there was a sound historical basis for this image there was also another side to the story. Some landlords, including the Duke of Manchester at Tandragee Castle, had bought seed rye privately and distributed it to their tenants. A number of landowners did decrease their rents or waive them altogether, such as Lord Rossmore, the Earl Erne and the Marquess of Ormonde. Sir George Staunton, owner of Clydagh, though an absentee, renounced his rents entirely, as did Henry O'Neill of Derrymacloughlin Castle, whose tenants showed their appreciation by lighting bonfires and dancing in his honour. Near Tuam, Mr Charles Cromie, of Annfield House, ordered his steward to ensure that all oats and grain grown on his property be ground and made into meal and flour for distribution to tenants.

Should I Stay or Should I Go?

Deep in their memory, the famine was still a painful experience for Irish people right through the nineteenth century and beyond. People used the words 'I'm famished' whenever they were cold or hungry, just one symptom of the lasting effect of the famine. Often, however, Irish people buried their memories of the famine deep in their subconscious. The time of the famine had been so horrific they just wanted to erase it from their memory. There was great shame attached to failing to feed one's family, and parents always blamed themselves for their children's deaths. Succeeding generations had inherited their shame. Even in the twentieth century, some people in rural Ireland would not travel anywhere without taking a piece of bread in their pocket because the fear of hunger was so strong.

In the years of their holocaust, the one ally ordinary people had was their faith. The Catholic faith was like a six-inch nail: the harder it was struck, the deeper it got entrenched into the timber. There was a story told about the Virgin Mary walking by a house in the West of Ireland on a stormy night. She and the child Jesus had no coat to protect them from the elements. As they passed, the woman of the house called them inside and gave Mary a bowl of nettle soup and an old sack to give extra cover to the child. Mary's final blessing was that the family line would always remain intact. They were one of the few families who survived the Great Hunger. A sign that God's favour rested on them was that their rooster did not crow 'cockadoodledoo' but rather cried out 'Mac na hóighe slán', or 'the Virgin's Son is risen'.

Irish people had the strength and resilience to outlast the Vikings, Cromwell the cursed and the Great Starvation. Hardship and degradation were often their second homes, but somehow they always pulled through. God was as close to these people and their joys and sorrows as was any other member of their family.

There were two main options open to these people: emigration, if

21

they could afford it, or the poorhouse/workhouse. In many respects people thought they were safer in their own place, the workhouses having a huge stigma attached to them. Like the infamous coffin ships, there was so much disease in the workhouse that to sign into the place was often to sign one's own death warrant. Generally the poorhouses postponed death for a short while but no more.

In the poorhouses and soup kitchens, families were separated from each other. All the men were housed in one section, the women in another. There were separate places for babies, young children, young girls and boys. Once a family went in they might never see each other again. There were strict rules about communication with another section. If one person broke the rules the whole family might be thrown out. Through speaking Irish, people could sometimes pass on messages without their masters knowing what was being said. In many ways the poorhouse was worse than jail. At least in jail you could get news to and from your family.

The workhouse retained strong connections with the famine. In the years of the Great Hunger, as a last resort it held out the prospect of survival but at an enormous cost in terms of human dignity and self-respect. The stigma attached to admission to the workhouses has no direct parallel in contemporary society. The legacy of the poorhouses is that there remains to this very day a reluctance on the part of some old people, particularly in rural Ireland, to be admitted into a hospital.

Emigration was resisted because mortality rates on the ships were alarmingly high. There was so much disease in those so-called 'coffin ships' that people's chances of surviving that long journey in such a weak state were remote. People by and large did not trust the sea. They all heard the stories of the American sailing ship *Stephen Whitney*. On a foggy December night in 1847 the ship, sailing on a voyage from America to Bristol, was wrecked off the Irish coast on Bolig Rinn na mBeann on the Western Calf Island. Within days 94 bodies were washed up on the beaches. Some people were desperate enough to try anything, but the majority preferred to meet their maker on their own land rather than on the other side of the Atlantic Ocean.

Nobody knows how many people went on the coffin ships. The one reliable statistic is about a group who went to Canada, where they all died of typhoid fever in a place called Grosse Ile, just outside Quebec City. Twelve thousand Irish people were buried in mass graves in Canada. They set out to make their mark in the new world but the only mark they made was in a grave, a people with no name. It was their final indignity.

While the adventurous and the comparatively wealthy continued to try and find their promised land in America, Canada and Australia, the majority of Irish emigrants made the shorter, safer and cheaper trip to England. They settled in clusters in cities like Manchester and Liverpool. What former President Mary Robinson terms 'the Irish diaspora' was born, and for generations of Irish people Manchester became a home from home. However, it would be a mistake to think that emigration began with the famine.

The Hibernian Connection

According to the acclaimed historian Roy Foster, 'Emigration is the great fact of Irish social history from the early nineteenth century.' It was a reluctant parting, as many song titles bear witness to, but essential not just to people's physical health but also to their emotional health, because, as W.B. Yeats memorably wrote, 'Too long a sacrifice can make a stone of the heart.' Although it is emigration to America and the hated coffin ships which have been the subject of investigation, much more important in numerical terms was emigration to the UK. This was the exodus of the extremely poor who could not afford even the cheapest boat to America. A trip from Drogheda to Liverpool in the steamer *Faugh a Ballagh* cost five shillings; in small sailing ships involved in the coastal trade the fare could be only half a crown, and a large export of coal from Cardiff to Cork enabled vessels to carry passengers on the return journey not simply at a very low cost but for nothing at all.

A large-scale exodus of Irish immigrants long preceded the famine. In 1841, 57,651 Irish seasonal workers found work in Britain, and throughout the early decades of the nineteenth century the number of permanent Irish immigrants to the UK increased steadily. The Great Famine triggered a sudden and spectacular increase in these figures, and between 1841 and 1861 the number of Irish in Britain more than doubled. In Birmingham in 1841 there were 4,683 Irish people – a figure which had risen to 11,832 in 1861, about 6 per cent of the borough's population.

The 1836 Royal Commission Report on 'the State of the Irish Poor in Great Britain' disclosed that 100,000 Irish-born people were living in Manchester. By 1841 a tenth of the population of Manchester was Irish, yet Manchester's experience of the famine immigration was a microcosm of that in other industrial towns. Manchester already had a notorious Irish slum, the infamous 'little Ireland' which Engels in his *Description of the Working Classes in England* (1845) described as 'the most disgusting spot of all'. The sudden influx of new Irish could not be accommodated, irrespective of the degree of overcrowding. The Registrar of a Manchester district wrote that the starving Irish were 'rambling about the streets in droves' looking for a bed for the night and something to eat. As late as November 1847, 5,000 Irish paupers were receiving relief each week, and a fever epidemic broke out which was still raging among the Irish in 1854.

Most of the men were unskilled and often had to take the jobs nobody else would touch. An 1835 *Report on the State of the Irish Poor in England* offers an invaluable insight into the types of occupation available to Irish people by providing a breakdown of the 7,500 Irish workers in Liverpool in 1835:

Mechanics	780
Brickworkers	270
Sugar boilers	200
Masons' labourers	350
Bricklayers' labourers	850
Chemical workers	600
Sawyers	80
Labourers in smithies and plasterers' yards	340
Lumpers about the docks	1,700
Porters employed in warehousing goods	1,900
Coal heavers and sundry	430
	————
	7,500
	————

Between 1801 and 1841 the population of Britain grew by about 60 per cent, but the large towns grew by almost 140 per cent. Individual towns grew even faster. Between 1770 and 1831 Manchester increased its size six times. Consequently, builders had to put up houses quickly, and in addition these houses had to be cheap, since many people could not afford to pay more than two shillings a week in rent. The problem was exacerbated by the fact that in the early nineteenth century local authorities had little power to interfere even if they had the inclination.

As they were free to do more or less whatever they wanted, builders packed as many houses as they could into the smallest possible spaces. They were able to save land by building their houses not only in terraces but back to back. Even worse were the courts which were supposed to be wide enough for a cart to pass through, but sometimes a man could touch the houses on both sides with his arms stretched out. In them the sun rarely shone, and the air was stale. Parks and gardens were virtually non-existent. Edwin Chadwick's famous 1842 *Report on the Sanitary Condition of the Labouring Population of Great Britain* described Manchester in the following way:

> There are no public walks or places of recreation by which the thousands of labourers or their families can relieve the tedium of their monotonous employment. Pent-up in a close, dusty atmosphere from half past five or six o'clock in the morning till seven or eight o'clock at night, from week to week, without change, without intermission, it is not to be wondered at that they fly to the spirit and beer shops and the dancing houses.
>
> Manchester is singularly destitute of these resources which conduce at once to health and recreation; with a teeming population she has no public walks or resorts for the community to snatch an hour's enjoyment.

In fact by 1846 Manchester was fortunate enough to be granted a park. It was the only English city with the exception of London to have one.

Builders sought to minimise their costs not only in terms of land but in terms of materials. Outside walls had no cavities to keep dampness and cold at bay and, even more shamefully, there were no damp-courses, so that moisture crept up the walls and dampness was rampant.

Sanitation was dreadful. Most people used a privy which took the form of a shed with a wooden seat inside, below which was a cesspit. When the cesspit was full, workmen emptied it manually and took the mess away in carts that dripped and leaked as they trundled through the streets. The smell this created was so foul that it was illegal to do it by day. Consequently, those who got this job were called 'night men'. Only the lowest of the low took such a job and they were not very diligent in the way they went about it.

Those lucky enough to have a sewer in their street still had sanitation problems. Frequently there were no drains connecting the house to the sewers, as these were costly and neither householders nor landlords wanted to pay for them. Builders seldom conducted a proper survey before constructing the sewers, so that they were level and could not drain. Manchester was one of the best-served towns in the country in this respect with 32 miles of sewers by 1830, but this still left nearly half the town without. In 1842 a doctor in the town observed:

> Whole streets, unpaved and without drains or main sewers, are worn into deep ruts and holes in which water constantly stagnates, and are so covered with refuse and excrementitious matter as to be almost impassable from depth of mud and intolerable from stench.

According to the census of 1841, 60 per cent of the inhabitants of the West of Ireland lived in what was termed fourth-class habitations, i.e. windowless single-roomed mud cabins with little or no furniture. It was from such areas that the majority of the Irish immigrants to Manchester came. They were singularly ill-equipped for city life and so desperate they were willing to take any job, however degrading, and to put up with any accommodation, regardless of the conditions. They went to towns like Manchester which could afford to provide poor relief.

The difficulty was that the local authorities were having a lot of problems coping with their indigenous poor. The arrival of huge numbers of 'pauper Irish' caused bitter resentment. All too often the Irish who had fled from starvation, eviction and poverty found that they had exchanged their squalor for a bed of sores in the stench of a cramped and overcrowded cellar in Manchester, St Giles or Glasgow. An 1851 report *On the Dwellings of the Poor* gives a vivid account of such overcrowding:

> Squalid children, haggard men with long uncombed hair, in rags with the short pipe in their mouths, many speaking Irish, women without shoes or stockings – a babe at the breast

with a single garment, confined to the waist by a bit of string; wolfish looking dogs; decayed vegetables strewing the pavement, low public houses, linen hanging across the street to dry . . . In one house a hundred persons have been known to sleep on a given night.

Wherever the Irish congregated in large quantities they found themselves driven to the very poorest lodgings and their living conditions were an accurate index of their poverty. Their living environment was shaped by forces over which they had little or no control. The lack of air and light which was such a common feature of much of their accommodation was largely the result of the tax on windows, which had caused landlords and tenants of large houses which had been turned into tenements or lodging houses to block up as many windows as possible. Consequently many of the staircases were so dark that people had to grope their way up them, at noonday as at night. It also led to dreadful ventilation.

Many of these dwellings were most unsuitable for use either as tenements or lodging houses and deteriorated rapidly because of overcrowding. This was especially the case with the cellar dwellings in which many of the Irish were found to be living in Manchester, Liverpool and the mill towns of Lancashire. Frequently these cellars had been condemned as unfit for human use but by the 1840s were again in full occupancy despite the fact that many of them were waterlogged and damp. A *Report on the State of Larger Towns* furnishes a graphic insight into the condition in which the Irish were forced to live in British cities in the middle of the century:

> Liverpool contains a multitude of inhabited cellars, close and damp, with no drain nor any convenience, and these pest houses are constantly filled with fever. Some time ago I visited a poor woman in distress. The wife of a labouring man, she had been confined only a few days and herself and infant were lying on straw in a vault, through the outer cellar, with a clay floor impervious to water. There was no light nor ventilation in it, and the air was dreadful. I had to walk on bricks across the floor to reach her bedside, as the floor itself was flooded with stagnant water . . . I found, about two years ago, a court of houses, the floors of which were below the public street, and the area of the whole court was a floating

mass of putrefied animal and vegetable matter, so dreadfully offensive that I was obliged to make a precipitate retreat. Yet the whole of the houses were inhabited!

Many of the cellars were originally intended as weaving shops and had been selected for that specific purpose as the dampness prevented the yarns breaking. With the decline in hand-loom weaving, the cellars were transformed into residences for labourers and factory workers. A report found that 39,000 people were living in cellars in Liverpool, 18,000 in Manchester and proportionate numbers in the smaller Lancashire towns.

The absence of ventilation and the damp and discomfort of these cellars was exacerbated by the overcrowding and lack of adequate furnishings. An investigation of the cellars in Manchester established that there were:

1,500 cases in which three persons slept in one bed;
738 cases in which four persons slept in one bed;
281 cases in which five persons slept in one bed;
94 cases in which six persons slept in one bed;
27 cases in which seven persons slept in one bed;
2 cases in which eight persons slept in one bed;
31 had no beds.

The Pluck of the Irish

A feature of Irish immigrants not just in Manchester but in all cities was that they tended to congregate in specific areas with cheap rooms for predominantly single men and women. In the main the Irish travelled from the known to the known. New arrivals sought out friends and relatives from the 'old place' for assistance in finding jobs and accommodation. Most of the large English cities such as London, Manchester, Birmingham and Coventry have particular localities with clusters of people from particular parts of Ireland. Hence by the middle of the nineteenth century the phrase 'Manchester's little Ireland' had gained popular currency.

Necessity was the mother of invention in this environment. One practice which was prevalent among poor families in the north was to store urine for laundering purposes. After it had been kept a sufficient time it was discovered to be an adequate substitute for soda. In Britain Irish immigrants began to adopt local customs.

Sedatives were used on children to keep them quiet during the day while their parents went out to work. In 1843 a druggist in Manchester claimed that there was hardly a family among the really poor who did not sedate their children. He went on to describe the practice in the following way:

> The mother goes out to her work in the morning, leaving her child either in the charge of a woman who cannot be trusted with it, or with another child of perhaps ten years old. A dose of 'quietness' is, therefore, given to the child to prevent it being troublesome. The child thus drugged sleeps, and may awaken at dinner time; so, when the mother goes out again, the child receives another dose. Well, the mother and father come home at night quite fatigued, and as they must rise early to begin work for the day, they must have sleep undisturbed by the child; so it is again drugged, and in this manner young children are often drugged three times in each day.

Whereas their Scottish and English neighbours used opiates mixed with sugar and water, the Irish were deeply inimical to such sedatives and induced the same effect with alcohol.

A further unsavoury practice was infanticide. An 1843 report was able to prove cases in Stockport and Manchester. It cost approximately £1 to bury a child but the burial clubs would pay between £3 and £5 on the death of an infant. As people could take out insurances in a number of different burial societies, the scope for profit was significant. Money would be allocated from the families' day-to-day needs to finance the insurance, and a premium was placed on the potential gain from the death of one member of the family, which effectively encouraged infanticide. A common phrase in Manchester among the poorer class of women in referring to a child was: 'Aye, aye, that child will not live, it is in the burial club.'

In the main, Irish immigrants would have found that life in Manchester was easier than in Ireland. Nonetheless their lives were far from agreeable. The men specialised in heavy construction work, moving around the country from site to site. Apart from the conventional labourers who did the digging and shovelling, there were the 'navvies', originally the 'navigators' who learnt their trade in the construction of waterways but who later found work in the making of railways and roads, who did the onerous and risky tasks like tunnelling. The Irish were desirable employees from the contractors' point of view because of their willingness to be constantly on the move. Family ties restricted the mobility of their British counterparts.

A surprisingly high number of Irishmen found jobs in the armed services. A few found fame and temporary and relative fortune as prize-fighters. Single Irish women found work as domestic servants.

Wages were low but Irish people earned more than they were used to at home. For this reason they were prepared to accept wages lower than native workers. This created tension, especially when Irish immigrants were used to break strikes. The Irish were seen by many as being drunken troublemakers. However, there were more objective voices. Commenting on the construction of the Caledonian Railway in 1846, Thomas Carlyle observed:

> The Yorkshire and Lancashire men, I hear, are reckoned the worst; and not without glad surprise I find the Irish are the best in point of behaviour. The postman tells me that several of the poor Irish do regularly apply to him for money drafts, and send their earnings home. The English, who eat twice as much beef, consume the residue in whisky and do not trouble the postman.

The reference to the postman is significant. Remittances home from Manchester were an important boost to the Irish economy, especially in some of the most deprived parts of the country. The attachment to home was probably one of the reasons why so few Irish workers got involved in working-class movements in England such as the Chartists. Bronterre O'Brien and Fergus O'Connor, two of the leaders of the Chartist movement, were Irish and very much the exception.

Another deviation from the norm was John Doherty. A native of Donegal, he emigrated to Manchester and was imprisoned after a strike in 1818. He was elected Secretary of Manchester Spinners' Union, which was surprising given his Irish Catholic background, and was their advocate before a Parliamentary Select Committee in 1838. He founded *The Conciliator*, or *Cotton Spinners' Weekly Journal*, and was Secretary of the Society for the Enforcement of the Factory Act and of the National Association for the Protection of Labour.

Hard Times

The British economy performed erratically after the Industrial Revolution, with periods of boom followed by periods of great recession. For many Irish immigrants the only option was a job in the mines, where conditions were very bleak. The 1842 Parliamentary Papers provide graphic evidence of the horrific conditions.

> I have often been shocked in contemplating the hideous and anything but human appearance of these men, who are generally found in a state of bestial nakedness, lying their whole length on the uneven floor, and supporting their heads upon a board or short crutch; or sitting upon one heel balancing their persons by extending the other. Black and filthy as they are in their low, dark, heated and dismal chambers, they look like a race fallen from the common stock. It did not much surprise me to be told that old age came prematurely upon them; indeed the careworn countenances, the grey hair and furrowed brows I met with at that age were sufficient indications of the fact.

Given their working conditions and poverty, many men sought refuge in drink. Drunkenness was the plague of the working classes. Public houses became ever more popular, and increased competition led owners to brighten and smarten up their establishments. Musicians were employed to add to the gaiety. Manchester was unique insofar as on Sundays psalms were played on organs.

Another response to working-class discontent surfaced as workers began to be replaced by machines: workers started to destroy their machines. Initially they were demolished on a random basis, but within a short time an organised campaign developed, conducted by a group called the Luddites. According to a legend – which probably does not stand up to the full rigours of historical scholarship – the group took its name from Ned Ludd, who was an apprentice who smashed his employer's equipment as revenge for a beating.

By 1812 the movement spread to Lancashire, where the hand-loom weavers exacted retribution on the power looms. There were riots in Manchester, raids on factories and wholesale demolition of steam looms. Secret committees were organised in the city, running the movement. In many parts of England the wide frames were scattered all over the countryside in private cottages, making them soft targets for the Luddites. In new cities like Manchester, however, the steam looms were in factories, so the workers had to attack them openly. Troops could easily defend the factories and it was easy to pick up the rioters. Many were brought to trial and transported, and two were hanged.

Radical groups sought to improve the condition of the working class. In 1819 the mob orator Henry Hunt went to St Peter's Fields, Manchester, to address 80,000 people at a time of trade depression. Although the meeting was quite orderly, a body of cavalry appeared and charged the crowd, trampling and sabring men, women and children. Eleven people were killed and hundreds more were injured in what became known as the Peterloo incident. The government replied by congratulating the magistrates who ordered the charge.

Children of a Lesser God

The bad working conditions were not simply confined to adults. Children too were shamefully exploited by unscrupulous factory owners. Not all employers were cruel, however. One of the exceptions was John Fielden, who was considered to be very sympathetic to working people because he ran his factory in a very humane way by the standards of the time. He was a Member of Parliament for Oldham and in order to get a better appreciation of the plight of working people arranged, with some other MPs, to meet a delegation of working people at Manchester. In his book *The Curse of the Factory System* Fielden wrote about his impressions of the meeting:

> One of the delegates gave a statement with particulars of a calculation of the number of miles which a child had to walk in a day in minding the spinning machine; it amounted to twenty-five! The statement excited great surprise: but this delegate was followed by another who had also made calculations. He calculated that a child has to walk twenty-four miles in the day: and, if the distance that it frequently has to walk to and from home be thrown in, it makes, not infrequently, a distance of nearly thirty miles.

Fielden was so shocked by what he heard that he went back to investigate conditions in his own factory and discovered that some of the children who worked for him walked nearly as far. John Brown provided a harrowing account of seven-year-old Robert Blincoe's first day in a factory:

> They reached the mill about half-past five. Blincoe heard a burring sound before he reached the portals, and smelt the fumes of the oil with which the axles of twenty-thousand wheels and spindles were bathed. The moment he entered the doors, the noise appalled him, and the stench seemed intolerable.
>
> The task first allotted to him was to pick up the loose cotton that fell upon the floor. Apparently nothing could be easier, and he set to it with diligence, although much terrified by the whirling motion and noise of the machinery, and not a little affected by the dust and flue with which he was half suffocated. Unused to the stench he soon felt sick, and by constantly stooping, his back ached. Blincoe therefore took the liberty to sit down: but this attitude, he soon found, was strictly forbidden. His task-master gave him to understand he must keep on his legs. He did so, till twelve o'clock, being six hours and a half without the least intermission. Blincoe suffered greatly with thirst and hunger.

The frightening thought was that at noon, this young boy had only completed half his day's work. In the factories, children's work was normally light and the chief problem was the long hours. However, in the mines conditions were much worse.

The youngest children in the mine were trappers. Throughout the mines there were doors that had to remain shut most of the time in order for the air to circulate to all the workings. A trapper sat at each of these doors and opened it with a piece of twine each time a load of coal came by. An 1842 Royal Commission that investigated the problem of child labour in the mines uncovered the following:

> The children that excite the greatest pity are those who stand behind the doors to open and shut them: they are called trappers, who in the darkness, solitude and stillness as of night, eke out a miserable existence for the smallest of wages. I can never forget the first unfortunate creature that I met

with: it was a boy of about eight years old, who looked at me
as I passed with an expression the most abject and idiotic –
like a thing, a creeping thing, peculiar to the place. On
approaching and speaking to him he shrank trembling and
frightened into a corner.

Children started working so young because their parents were
normally unable to support the family by themselves. Moreover,
the coming of machinery created many easy jobs which children
could do for meagre wages. It did not make sense for the factory
owners to employ adults for much higher wages. In some cases
children began working in the factories at the age of five.

Yet a further serious problem was the cruelty of the factory
owners. If children did not perform up to scratch they were
normally beaten. Most factories employed an overlooker who
would monitor the children and walked around with a strap to
administer 'punishment' as he deemed appropriate. In the mines
beatings were often even more severe. Primary source evidence
suggests that a standard approach was to hold the boy's head
between his knees while the others took turns to give him several
strokes on the bare bottom with a plank. The nail-makers of Sedgley
went a step further. When a bar of white-hot iron was taken out of
the furnace it was covered with hundreds of tiny particles.
Normally the workmen shook them to the ground, but if he wanted
to punish children he would shower the sparks all over them. This
was known as sending a 'flash of lightning'.

Given the long hours, it was inevitable that such young children
would fall asleep on the job. In the final few hours, particularly on
dark winter's days, it was very difficult for the children to sustain
their concentration. A severe beating to one child served the
purpose not only of ensuring the boy in question kept awake for the
rest of his shift, but more importantly of providing a forceful
reminder to his colleagues that they too could not afford to slacken
off. The 1842 Royal Commission reported:

I would draw your attention to the passive and uncom-
plaining nature of the evidence taken from so many children
and young persons in painful circumstances. I cannot but
consider this in itself as evidence of their low and depressed
condition – the poverty of their spiritual and moral nature.

> Many of these poor children, deposing that they worked from twelve to fourteen hours a day for 1s 6d or 2s 6d a week, not a penny of which they had for their own use, and often without any regular hours for their meals; who were clothed in rags; who acknowledged that they felt often sick or otherwise ill, and that they had not enough to eat – who were sometimes 'beaten badly', but who 'only felt it for a day or two' – have still replied that they 'liked their work', 'were well-treated', 'were only punished when they deserved it', etc. They evidently knew of nothing else but to wake and go to work from day to day, and to continue working until permitted to leave off. Such a question as 'Do you feel tired?' had never been asked them, and they did not understand it.

Children in Manchester did have one champion in (Sir) Dr James Kay Shuttleworth. His family name was Kay but, being perhaps the first ever 'new man', he changed his name when he married Janet Shuttleworth in 1842. Kay studied medicine at Edinburgh and went on to practise in Manchester, where his preoccupation was the welfare of the working classes. He became Medical Officer to the Ancoats and Ardwick Dispensary, and Secretary to the Manchester Board of Health. In the early days his chief concern was the cholera epidemic, and what this taught him about the poor compelled him to write a book, *Moral and Physical Condition of the Working Classes Employed in the Cotton Manufacture in Manchester*.

Kay felt that most of the problems of the poor could be attributed to lack of education. While there were schools in Manchester, the level of education was poor because the teachers were poor. Kay found the solution on a trip to Holland, where teachers served an apprenticeship, as they did in industry. A promising student aged about 14 was apprenticed to a master and, in the same way that the apprentice craftsman did simple tasks for the employer, the apprentice teacher performed simple tasks in the classroom, progressing steadily to the more complicated. In 1839 Shuttleworth became Secretary of the newly formed Committee of Council for Education. It helped to establish the idea of elementary education for all as an essential part of social policy. While politicians were resistant to the idea of the State having a duty to provide education, in 1870 an Education Act aimed to provide a school place for every child in the country.

On the Outside Looking in

It was the crushing weight of economic necessity which compelled huge numbers of Irish people to take the boat to England. However, they did not easily integrate into the social fabric. This created a certain amount of suspicion, and they were often seen as a threat to the political system. This fear was fuelled by the presence of subversive societies such as the Fenians and the Irish Republican Brotherhood on English soil in the latter part of the nineteenth century. *Punch* cartoons of the time depicted the Irishman either as a comic peasant, 'Paddy', or, more sinisterly, as an ape-like animal. Occasionally the two caricatures were blended in a cartoon of a mischievous chimpanzee.

The fact that Irish immigrants had no experience of urban living meant that they found it very difficult to make the transition to live in cities like Manchester. In very many cases they continued to live in the English city as they had done in their Irish village. Housing conditions in the UK were poor enough already, but the huge influx of Irish immigrants added petrol to the flames. There was widespread disgust with their tendency to keep chickens, goats, pigs, donkeys and dogs with them in their crowded accommodation. Writing about Manchester in 1846, the German commentator Engels's portrait of an Irishman was less than flattering:

> [He] builds a pigsty against the house wall as he did at home, and if he is prevented from doing this, he lets the pig sleep in the room with himself . . . . The Irishman loves his pig as the Arab his horse, with the difference that he sells it when it is fat enough to kill. Otherwise he eats and sleeps with it, his children play with it, ride upon it, roll in the dirt with it, as anyone may see a thousand times repeated in all the great towns of England.

Another of the factors that came together like converging lines to fuel English prejudice against Irish immigrants was that the Irish were Roman Catholics. This is despite the fact that minute analysis of Irish Catholics in nineteenth-century Manchester discovered them only 'marginally more faithful in church attendance than working-class people of other denominations'. Anti-Catholic feeling was still strong in the nineteenth century, with the Roman Church regularly denounced as 'the Scarlet Woman'. Catholicism was seen as incompatible with patriotism, as Catholics' first allegiance was to the Pope. An editorial in 1853 in *The Times* captured this feeling: 'We very much doubt whether in England, or indeed in any free Protestant country, a true Papist can be a good subject.' One incident sums up the close identification with Catholicism. In 1848 the murder by an Irish navvy of a young Welshman in Cardiff led to a mob attack on the Catholic church and priest's house there. The fact that the police took no action to protect the property of the Irish or to arrest the rioters spoke volumes about British attitudes.

Against this backdrop the Irish became the scapegoats for many of the social problems of the time. There were loud calls for a restriction on the number of Irish who could be admitted to England. A flavour of the discussion comes from an article in *The Cardiff Advertiser and Merthyr Guardian* in April 1849 which was titled 'The Irish Plague'.

> Upwards of 50 Irish wretches, in a most deplorable plight, were landed on Penarth beach and proceeded on to Cardiff. Some check must be put to the thousands of Irish paupers who flock into the country.

The weight of public pressure forced the government to take drastic action. A Bill was introduced into Parliament and rushed through both Houses, giving municipal authorities powers to send Irish paupers back to Ireland with the bare minimum of legal formality and delay. Five days after it became law, Dublin received an initial consignment of 200 returned paupers. The Irish Under-Secretary T.N. Redington observed: 'The Lord Mayor seems puzzled what to do with them.' Destitute people actually suffering from fever were dispatched back to Ireland. The Mayor of Drogheda complained bitterly to the Home Office that the Liverpool authorities had sent five pauper fever cases who were too sick to stand down to the docks in a cart, and forced them on board.

Significantly, Karl Marx compared the attitude of the English worker to the Irish immigrants with that of the 'poor whites' to the 'niggers' in the southern states of the USA. Marx recognised that the main reason for the English working man's distrust was that the Irish were a threat to their economic well-being. The Irish were portrayed as a threat to the British way of life because of their lack of 'civilisation' which would drag down the British to their drunken, riotous level. It is striking that the only issue which transcended the class boundaries of British society was abhorrence of Irish immigrants. These opinions found ready outlets in the British media. In March 1850 *The Cardiff Advertiser and Merthyr Guardian* observed:

> We are accustomed to associate notions of filth, squalor and beggarly destitution with everything Irish from the large number of lazy, idle and wretched natives of the Sister Island who are continually crossing our paths.

Even in the twentieth century it was not uncommon in Birmingham, Manchester and parts of London to find notices offering accommodation that specified 'No coloured; no Irish'. Trawling through the reports of such naked racism in the summer of 1997 was like travelling through a time warp. It was interesting to hear some of the exact same arguments, emotions, insults and language mirrored in the discussion about refugees coming to Ireland which had formed part of the agenda in the 1997 General Election. Many of the Irish who arrived in Manchester in the 1840s would have found common cause with the Bosnians who arrived in Dublin 150 years later.

Chapter Three

More Than a Game

Interviewer: 'Was there much TB then?'
Manchester United fan of the 1920s: 'No, but we had radio.'

In his prologue to *The Go-Between*, L.P. Hartley wrote: 'The past is a foreign country: they do things differently here.' Before the famine, emigration was anathema to most Irish people. Lord Stanley, later Earl of Derby, remarked in 1845: 'The warm attachment of the Irish peasant to the locality where he was born and brought up will always make the best and most carefully conducted scheme of emigration a matter of painful sacrifice for the emigrant.'

The famine caused a temporary change to that pattern as hundreds of thousands of people willingly left the country because to remain was to sign their death warrant. As economic conditions improved, the aversion to emigration returned. Throughout much of the twentieth century the spectre of young people taking the emigrant's ship in the West of Ireland, in many cases never to return, precipitated weeping and wailing and shrieks of anguish which also marked the 'keening' for the dead.

Frequently the Irish brought a lot of ideological baggage with them. In politics the difference in interests between Irish immigrants and their Mancunian neighbours was obvious; for the immigrant the prevailing concerns of Irish nationalism and the Roman Catholic Church played a crucial part. Native workers seldom shared these concerns. Such was the Catholic Church's opposition to trade unions that some bishops even went so far as to command that communion be denied to those who belonged to 'illegal secret societies'. This approach did not cut much ice in the building trades, with Irishmen to the forefront of bricklayers' clubs in England.

Post-famine the Irish national pulse was strengthening perceptibly. The demand for self-government was being made with more vigour. Political structures were not as secure as they had been, and the old establishment was being challenged in various ways. In the countryside the stirrings could be seen among the tenant farmers.

Throughout rural Ireland, agrarian unrest accelerated with increasing demands for tenant right reforms. Landlords were seen as a privileged minority, alienated from the majority of their tenants by differences in both religion and politics. Tenants normally held their holdings from year to year, thus having no security. In times of bad harvests many could not afford to pay the rent. A high number of landlords were absentees living outside the country and leaving the management of their estates to agents. The great disaster of the famine was followed by mass evictions of tenants. The need for reform of the system was becoming more obvious in the years that followed.

The Fenian Rising took place on 5 March 1867. The plan was for guerilla units to assemble in different parts of Ireland, with a concentration around Dublin and the south-west. Rail and telegraph communications were to be sabotaged and police barracks assaulted, and the government was to be tormented until the Irish republic would receive a major aid package from America. The rising was a total disaster. The Fenians had a handful of minor successes, capturing two police barracks in the greater Dublin region, at Stepaside and Glencullen. Rebels also captured a police barracks at Knockadoon in County Cork.

Typical of the Fenian experiences was the rising in Ballyhurst, near Tipperary town. An Irish-American civil war veteran named Bourke was in charge. He had a shrunken leg and led his men mounted on a horse. Initially he and his troop had successfully destroyed telegraph poles and torn up railway lines. When British soldiers approached the earthworks, however, the Fenians fired one round of shots and fled, as Bourke galloped off in a different direction screaming: 'To the mountains! To the mountains!' As the snow fell, Bourke did not even make the mountains. His horse was shot and he was caught limping by a hedge.

Interestingly, the contents of his pocket revealed: a Catholic prayer book, photographs of some girls, a prescription for an eye infection, a railway guide and a new oath to be administered to the civilian population in the event of victory. At no stage did it look like the new oath would be needed.

The Manchester Martyrs

Like the 1916 rising, the Fenian Rising was more significant for its sequel than the event itself. There was a debate among the Fenians about what to do next. The influential O'Donovan Rossa advocated 'carrying' the war into Britain, though he was in the minority. The Irish-American veteran Colonel T.J. Kelly, the main figure in the Fenians, was in England. On 11 September 1867, the police arrested two men in Manchester who had been behaving suspiciously in a doorway. They said their names were Wright and Williams and they were remanded on a charge of loitering. An informer told the police that they were Kelly and Captain Deasy, a leading figure in the rising in County Cork.

The following week, as an unescorted prison van was bringing Kelly and Deasy in handcuffs from the police court in Manchester to Belle Vue prison it was stopped and surrounded by about 30 Fenians who had been lying in wait for it. Some of them, armed with revolvers, forced the unarmed police on the outside of the van to get down and kept bystanders away while others tried to force open the locked van and rescue the two Fenians from the cells inside.

Inside the van, apart from Kelly and Deasy and a motley crew of criminals, was Police Sergeant Brett who, called upon through the ventilator of the locked back door to surrender, forcefully declined to do so. This prompted one Fenian, knowing that the police were not far away, to fire his revolver through the ventilator, though whether to kill or simply scare the sergeant or just to break open the door is not known. The bullet mortally wounded the policeman, and one of the female criminals removed the keys from the dying man's hands and threw them out through the ventilator. Moments later Kelly and Deasy, complete with handcuffs, escaped over a wall and across the railway line – never to be recaptured.

One of the personalities involved in the rescue was John O'Connor Power (1848-1919). He was born in County Galway, emigrated to Rochdale and became active in the Irish Republican Brotherhood. In 1874 he became an MP for Mayo and became the first MP to join the Land League in 1879.

On 23 November 1867 three men were executed for Sergeant Brett's death. Their names, Allen, Larkin and O'Brien, entered the lexicon of Irish heroes. They were described as the 'Manchester Martyrs' and their statues became part of republican iconography. Back in Ireland, Archbishop MacHale of Tuam and the greatest thorn in the side of the leader of the Catholic Church in Ireland, Cardinal Paul Cullen, officiated at a high Mass for the 'martyrs'. Support for the Fenian question was a pawn in the power game which was being played out between Cullen and MacHale.

Ten years later the Manchester martyrs were the subject of an interesting exchange in the House of Commons. The Chief Secretary for Ireland referred to 'the Manchester murders'. He was brought to a sudden halt by a cry of 'No! No!' from the Irish benches. In a flurry of moral indignation the Chief Secretary continued: 'I regret that there is any Honourable Member in this House who will apologise for murder.'

A tall, handsome Cambridge graduate who was a Protestant landowner and a member for County Meath coolly rose to his feet and answered: 'The Right Honourable Gentleman looked at me so directly when he said that he regretted that any member should apologise for murder that I wish to say as publicly and as directly as I can that I do not believe, and never shall believe, that any murder was committed at Manchester.'

The MP, Charles Stewart Parnell, went on to become the most famous man in Ireland and a leading player on the British political stage. His meteoric rise to power was matched only by his fall after one of the greatest sexual scandals in the history of politics when he fell in love with a married woman, Mrs Kitty O'Shea.

Roots

Paradoxically, while most Irish immigrants were anxious to protect their national identity in foreign fields, they were also anxious to blend in their new environment. Sport, particularly football, provided the perfect outlet, and long before the term was coined it was 'politically correct' to do so. Other avenues towards social integration such as joining the local branch of the Conservative Party would have incurred social leprosy. Thus for Irish immigrants in Manchester at the end of the nineteenth century, football assumed a deep sociological significance.

Neville Cardus was writing of his beloved cricket when observing that 'a great game is part of the nation's life and environment; it is indeed an organism in an environment . . . as our great game is inevitably an expression in part of our spiritual and material condition as a nation and a people, it must go through metamorphoses; it must shed skins and grow new ones . . .'. Cardus could have been writing about football in the latter years of the nineteenth century. The times they were a-changing.

In 1895 the superb all-round athlete, cricketer and footballer C.B. Fry donned the mantle of social commentator when he remarked: 'The great and widespread interest in football is a manifest fact. So much so that nowadays it is frequently urged that cricket can no longer be regarded as our "national game" in the true sense of the word. Football, it is claimed, has now the first place in the popular heart.'

To modern eyes Fry's comments might appear curious. However, for much of the 1800s football was alien to the lives of industrial workers. Time off work was minimal apart from Sundays, and holidays or leisure activities were considered inappropriate for the Lord's day. The only formal holidays were at Easter and Christmas. If sport was to emerge as a significant feature in the lives of working-class people, significant economic changes were essential. Campaigns to improve life for workers began to reap their harvest in the 1840s. An important milestone came in 1850 with the Factory Act which introduced a 60-hour week for women.

However, the most crucial development was the so-called *semaine anglaise* which provided workers with a free Saturday afternoon. The textile industry was the first to introduce this concession, but by the 1860s it had become commonplace. This allowed the industrial labour force to spend their free afternoons in the pursuit of structured recreation. Moreover, working men now found that they had more money to spend as in real terms their wages rose appreciably from the 1850s onwards.

This development was not to everyone's taste. In 1863 the *Illustrated London News* complained that: 'There is, perhaps, no social problem more difficult of solution than that which involves the affording of more holidays to the working classes without at the same time diminishing their means of subsistence.' In a flurry of moral indignation in 1871 *The Times* bemoaned 'an increasing tendency of late years among all classes to find excuse for Holydays'. That same year the first ever bank holiday was introduced. The Bank Holiday Act boldly went where no legislation had gone before, transforming old religious holidays into secular days of recreation sanctioned by the State. This was much to the chagrin of *The Times* which stubbornly continued to call such days 'holydays'. The first such bank holiday witnessed unprecedented chaos at the railway stations and steamboat piers.

By the end of the nineteenth century, football had become the sport of the industrial working class – a major social change. This was reflected in the remarks of a Manchester industrialist in 1881, reminiscing on life in the city in the 1830s: 'As for a Saturday afternoon holiday, it was not even dreamt of. Hence people had fewer opportunities of indulging their inclinations in this direction.'

While workers saw football as a leisure activity, others saw it as an opportunity to pursue another agenda. Clergymen viewed it as an ideal antidote to urban degeneracy. Vigorous physical activity would benefit the young on every level including the spiritual which led to a proliferation of football teams associated with working-class churches. By 1880 83 of the 344 football clubs in Birmingham and by 1885 25 of the 112 clubs in Liverpool had religious affiliations. Some of the top teams of today began life as church teams, including Aston Villa, Birmingham City, Bolton Wanderers, Blackpool, Everton, Fulham, Liverpool, Southampton, Swindon and Wolves. Schools too got in on the act, and Blackburn Rovers, Chester, Leicester City, Queen's Park Rangers and Sunderland owe their origins to particular schools.

The local authority in Manchester was one of the first to introduce new municipal parks in an effort to introduce a shaft of light into the greyness of their industrial city which enabled the masses to play football. The game's new popularity was reflected in the growth of working-class kit. In 1880 Lewis's of Manchester sold knickerbockers at 6s 9d, jerseys for 3s 11d – and hand-sewn footballs for 10s 6d.

A Sporting Genesis

The factory floor itself spawned a number of football teams. In a northern suburb of Manchester, employees at the carriage and wagon department of the Lancashire and Yorkshire Railway Company established the Newton Heath team in 1878 at their depot. Initially their name was Newton Heath (LYR), but they dropped the initials LYR as the club gained more popularity and expanded its activities, recruiting players from outside the local railway yard. Twenty-four years later, following the club's bankruptcy, they took the name Manchester United. The club first joined the Football League (as members of the First Division) in 1892 and have never since dropped out of the top two divisions.

From the very beginning, Irish players were at the heart of United's playing staff. John Penden became Ireland's first professional footballer when he joined Newton Heath. Tommy Morrison made history on Christmas Day 1902 when he became the first Irishman to wear the colours of Manchester United in a league derby match against City. The following day Morrison went one better when he became the first Irishman to score a league goal for the club. Two years later he earned the distinction of becoming the first Irishman to score for United (against Notts County) in an FA Cup tie.

For immigrants in particular, football was more than a game – it was an integral part of people's identity. The Irish immigrants were by and large a placid, charitable bunch. They were a contented, resourceful people enshrined in a devout and peaceful religious society, dwelling in an austere environment where, in order to be self-supporting, they had to work hard. Their tastes were simple and their needs modest. History endowed them with an amazing sense of community. This in turn nurtured a tradition of great goodwill and generosity, an awareness of other people's difficulties and a readiness to help in times of adversity. They were patient up to a point but did not want the hostility that they had experienced throughout the 1860s and '70s to continue.

The thirst for social inclusion was most keenly felt by the handful of Irish immigrants with aspirations to move in the upper echelons of Mancunian society. The first Irish were brought over to Manchester by the De Traffords, a Catholic family, who made the journey as a consequence of religious persecution during the Reformation. The De Traffords were the most influential landowners in the area and owned the ground which would become the theatre of dreams, Old Trafford. They attracted the Irish intelligentsia in the shape of such professionals as doctors and lawyers who would almost without exception rise to prominence in their adopted city.

Manchester United fans, indigenous and imported, were united on the terraces in a common cause regardless of class, nationality or creed. Football was a badge of identity which enabled Irish immigrants to consider themselves as Mancunians. Attendance at a United fixture was a social rite of passage for any Irishman with ambitions to fit into the local community.

The bonds of loyalty between the Irish and United were considerably strengthened as the Reds began to taste the fruits of success. In 1907–08 and in 1910–11 United won the league title and in 1909 they beat Bristol City to win the FA Cup for the first time, courtesy of a goal from Sandy Turnbull and a fine performance from Billy Meredith. Five years earlier Turnbull had picked up his first FA Cup medal when he helped Manchester City defeat Bolton 1–0, as had Meredith, who scored City's winning goal in the final. Turnbull was killed in action on the battlefields of France on 3 May 1917.

Meredith's name is always linked with that of Stanley Matthews in discussion of the all-time-great outside-rights. Meredith, though, was a more prolific scorer than Matthews, scoring almost 200 league and cup goals in over 700 appearances in his 30-year career. In 1924 the hallowed Welsh wizard of the right wing played in his last cup match, a semi-final during his second stint at Manchester City, when he was 49 years and eight months old and remains the oldest player ever to line out in the competition proper. He won 48 caps over a 25-year period.

Meredith was something of an *enfant terrible* in the eyes of the football authorities. In 1905 he was embroiled in initially bribes and then an illegal-payment scandal that led to him being suspended by the FA. The affair almost ruined City. At Old Trafford Meredith teamed up with United's captain Charlie Roberts and became a strident campaigner in the battle to get the Players' Union recognised by the FA and Football League. The controversy lingered for 18 months and during the summer of 1909, a short time after the cup victory, those players were briefly suspended by the FA.

An important milestone occurred on Saturday, 19 February 1910 when United moved into their new home at Old Trafford. United's previous grounds at North Road and Bank Street had both been well short of the desired standard, and following their league and cup successes the club decided on a move to a new stadium, one that had been specially built for them, and that would match their footballing triumphs. The stadium was designed by Archibald Leitch, the acclaimed architect of a number of football grounds. It was intended to be the biggest ground in the country, with the most lavish of facilities for players and staff.

The site was purchased with a £60,000 grant from the chairman John Davies, but as construction costs rocketed by an additional £30,000, some of the planned facilities had to be significantly scaled down. Instead of 100,000 the capacity was reduced to 70,000, and some of the plans for office facilities had to be shelved. The first game was against Liverpool. An estimated 50,000 paid to see the match. It is said that a few thousand more were sneaked in free of charge when gatemen, unable to cope with the queues, simply opened the doors.

In 1911 the FA Cup final replay was played at the ground in front of 56,000 spectators, Bradford City defeating Newcastle 1–0. Four years later Old Trafford was chosen as the venue for the FA Cup final itself, Sheffield United going on to beat Chelsea, as Crystal Palace had been turned into a military camp. The 1915 final was called 'the khaki final' as so many soldiers in uniform were among the crowd.

An Irish player was quickly destined to wear the United colours in the new stadium, Mickey Hamill joining United from Belfast Celtic for a record fee of £175. The outbreak of war in 1914 saw him return to his native city having made the centre-half position his own at Old Trafford. On Valentine's Day that same year he wrote himself into the history books at Middlesbrough by captaining the first Irish team to defeat England on English soil. After the war ended he joined Celtic, going on to win a league medal there. In 1920 he returned to Manchester – but this time with Manchester City.

Patriot Games

The fact that Irish immigrants quickly identified so freely with United and so easily with their new neighbours on the terraces is something of a surprise given that the historical enmity between Britain and Ireland continues to distort the sporting relationship between the countries even today.

An example of Irish sports fans' tendency to put the English in their place is their fondness for a story which pokes fun at the English cricket team. A young boy's parents were in the process of being divorced. The judge asked him:

'Would you like to live with your father?'
'No, he beats me.'
'So you would like to live with your mother?'
'No, she beats me.'
'Well, who would you like to live with?'
'The English cricket team – they can beat nobody!'

Even the Irish clergy succumb to the temptation to poke fun at English sport. A recent example of their holy wit is a story set in darkest Africa where there was a river infested with crocodiles. On the other side there was a tribe which various missionaries wanted to convert. However, nobody was willing to take the risk of crossing the river. In 1993 along came a group of Irish priests who waded across the river without coming to any harm. Shortly after they revealed their secret. 'We wore T-shirts bearing the words "England – World Cup Champions 1994". And sure, not even a crocodile was willing to swallow that!'

In from the Cold

Irish people were and are passionate about sport. It is said that in France you could win your country's national cycling tour seven times and walk the streets in anonymity. However, even win a stage once in Ireland and you are assured heroic status for a lifetime.

For the Irish working class, watching football at Old Trafford provided an escape from their problems and anxieties. There were other distractions too, such as Manchester's thriving theatrical tradition. Beckett put on a number of his first nights in Manchester. Another enrichment of Manchester's rich cultural tapestry was Mike Costello, of Irish extraction. He gained celebrity status as the great Blondini when he was buried in a coffin for 78 days for a £500 bet. One of his favourite escapades was to place himself in an ordinary coffin which was blown apart by dynamite.

Football, though, was the battery that drove Irish immigrants' imaginative lives and dared them to see themselves in a very different light – as pillars of the Manchester community. It allowed them to dream of better days to come. Success, albeit by association, such as watching United winning the title increased their self-esteem. They walked that little bit taller, they talked just a little more boldly, and they mingled among their new neighbours with pride. Football was their passport to social inclusion. In this way sport fulfilled its historic role of unifying people and acting as a counterweight to narrow sectional interests.

Chapter Four

MATTer of Fact

'Now listen, boys, I'm not happy with our tackling. We're hurting them but they keep getting up.'

— JIMMY MURPHY

The inter-war years were not happy ones for United. They failed to win any major honours and with few outstanding players they were relegated in 1921, 1931 and 1937. Some of their business dealings during these years were unorthodox, to put it mildly. In 1922 they signed Frank Barson, considered to be one of the toughest centre-halves to play for United, for £5,000, with the promise of a pub should United be promoted. They were, but there was such a charge when the pub doors were first opened that Barson had a change of heart and decided to forsake the life of a publican.

In the 1930s United were in serious financial difficulties, which explains why they hovered on the brink of relegation to the Third Division at one point, requiring a win in the final game of the season against Millwall to retain their tenure in Division Two. They were promoted back into Division One in 1936, thanks in no small part to 23 goals from Scottish international George Mutch. They crashed back to the Second Division the following year.

Keeper of the Flame

The 1930s brought a young goalkeeper to Old Trafford who would go on to have an influence on the club surpassed only by an élite few such as Matt Busby and Jimmy Murphy. Billy Behan joined United in 1933 from Shamrock Rovers and had one season in Manchester. His solitary league appearance at Old Trafford came in a 2–1 victory over Bury in March 1933. A brother-in-law of manager Scott Duncan sent him over to United for a month's trial.

Behan was a native of Ringsend, which was a remarkable place – and very different from today's incarnation. It was then a fishing village. Local man 'Spud' Murphy-Kearney was an internationally famous boat-builder. Billy's father, William, was known as the Grand Old Man of the fishermen of Ringsend. His speciality was drift nets which worked by tying one end on to a buoy, drawing the net across to the shore and leaving it there all night. In one go he caught 132 salmon. The record, though, was by a man called Hawkins, who caught 284 salmon and delivered them to Clontarf in a dog cart. Industrialisation and the consequent pollution, however, condemned the local fishing industry to a slow, painful death. Most of the fishing was done in a stretch of water that is now reclaimed land and owned by the shipping companies.

Before this, however, Ringsend was looked upon as a village, and not considered part of Dublin city. It can be said to be the cradle of Irish football, given the number of soccer internationals it has spawned and the intense rivalry it generated between two of the top sides in Irish soccer, Shamrock Rovers and Shelbourne.

Rovers were at the heart of Ringsend, whereas Shelbourne claimed the loyalty of the people living on its fringes such as Bath Avenue and Pearse Street. Shelbourne's foothold in the area would have increased had they availed of the opportunity to buy the present-day Shelbourne Park from Kennedy's bakery, but instead the greyhound aficionados snapped it up. Rovers actually got their name from Shamrock Avenue in Ringsend. At the time they were riding on the crest of a wave powered by the famous '4 Fs'.

Behan shared some of his memories of his time at Old Trafford with his son Terry.

> Every Friday the players waited with bated breath for their wages. They never knew if they would be paid or not until the man came back from the bank. Then a man called James Gibson came along and invested a lot of money in the club, and they never looked back after that.

Behan returned from Manchester to Ireland to play initially with Shelbourne and later with Shamrock Rovers, where he began an unusual FAI Cup trilogy when he won a winner's medal with the Hoops in 1936. He subsequently went on to manage a cup-winning team, Drumcondra, in 1954, and refereed another cup final after becoming a fully qualified FIFA referee.

The turning point in United's fortunes came in November 1937 when they beat Chesterfield 7–1 and began a run that took them to promotion. Part of that side was Henry, or Harry, Baird, who arrived at Old Trafford from Linfield in 1937, making his début for the club against Sheffield Wednesday. He went on to score 18 goals in his 53 games for United before leaving for Huddersfield Town the following year. Somewhat surprisingly, he won no caps for Northern Ireland in his United days. Injury and the great war threatened his career, but he went on to make 234 appearances for Ipswich Town.

Another Irishman who helped United gain promotion in 1938 was Tommy Breen, who joined the club in 1936. His career began with Newry and, like Packie Bonner, he originally played Gaelic football, where he learned the skills of safe handling and long kicking. Later he moved to Belfast Celtic, where he won four international caps and two Irish League Championship medals, before moving from Celtic Park to Old Trafford. He opened his league campaign in England in most inauspicious circumstances: after less than a minute of his début against Leeds at Elland Road he had to pick the ball out of the net.

He was United's sixth goalkeeper in six seasons and went on to make 71 appearances for the club between 1936 and 1938, helping them to win promotion after a season in Division Two. Following this success, however, he gave way to John Breedon. The outbreak of war saw Tommy leave Old Trafford to return to Belfast Celtic, and after the war he went south to play for Shamrock Rovers. He played for both Irish international sides.

Sporting Ecumenism

1937 also saw the début of one of United's most famous Irish players, Johnny Carey. In his early teens Carey showed great promise as a Gaelic footballer, but in the era of 'the ban' he was prohibited from playing 'foreign games'. The ban was a serious business. In 1943 one of the GAA's most illustrious sons, former

Taoiseach Jack Lynch, had been suspended for three months for attending a rugby match.

This lack of sporting ecumenism would endure for another generation. Liam Brady was expelled from his Christian Brothers school for playing soccer. In fairness, it must be acknowledged that the relationship between the GAA and the Catholic Church was also a complex one. Although culturally and in many respects spiritually they were very close and the Catholic Church was to the forefront in promoting the GAA, the Church banned its priests and seminarians from actually playing inter-county football. Priests therefore assumed names to allow their footballing careers to continue at the highest level. Everybody knew who they were, including usually the local bishop, often a fanatical GAA supporter, and a blind eye was turned. It was a Jesuitical solution to a uniquely clerical problem, despite the curious irony of men who preached the truth practising deception.

Carey came to United by accident. In 1936 United's chief scout, Louis Rocca, had been chasing Bohemians star Benny Gaughan. When he went over to Dublin to sign Gaughan he was told that a £200 under-the-counter payment would be required. Rocca promised to return with the money the following week. In the interim, though, Glasgow Celtic swooped for Gaughan with a fee of £300. Rocca was disappointed when he returned to Dublin, and turned to Billy Behan for consolation. Behan told him of an even better player in Dublin and brought him to see Johnny Carey play a starring role for St James's Gate. Rocca signed him on the spot for £250. He was almost the last player signed in Scott Duncan's five-year reign as United manager. It was a time when the opportunities for a young man like Carey were limited in a country where, in the words of James Joyce, 'Christ and Caesar were fist in glove'.

Born in February 1919, Carey was a product of the famous Home Farm assembly line of talented youngsters. At the tender age of 18 he made his United début in a 2-1 defeat at the hands of Southampton. Carey was probably the bargain buy of all time. Off the field he was the perfect gentleman, but on the field he was a tough, stylish defender. He began as an inside-forward but during the war was turned into a full-back.

John Joseph Carey was the definitive model professional. When war broke out he didn't take the soft option and return to neutral Ireland, but instead opted to volunteer for action with the Allies. The decision might appear surprising, given his patriotism and life-

53

long interest in the Irish language. There was, however, something of a split-level phenomenon in Irish attitudes to the war. Two contrasting parables serve to illustrate.

The Land of a Thousand Welcomes

In 1945, over 300 people attended the founding meeting of the Save the German Children Society in the Shelbourne Hotel. The motivations of these people were mixed. Dr Kathleen Murphy, a paediatrician, was appointed chairwoman. She claimed that they were concentrating on German people as they were the most 'necessitous', and that as Christians they were obliged to assist 'starving German children'.

However, others had a very different motive. An army officer confessed that he supported the society on the grounds of his pro-German feelings and his hatred of Britain. Another individual asserted that they should help the children because Ireland's freedom had been won with German guns.

The tenure of those remarks drew considerable odium on the Save the German Children Society. Following this meeting the British authorities branded the society fascist and indicated that they would only work with the Irish Red Cross. At the time most of the German children lived in the province of North Rhine Westphalia, which was under British rule.

On 27 July 1946, 88 German children emerged from a passenger ferry and tentatively set foot on Dun Laoghaire Pier. Waiting for them was a host of Red Cross workers with parcels of food, keeping up a stream of conversation, chattering excitedly and laughing. They were accompanied by groups of nervous families who were seeking out the girl or boy who would eventually become their temporary child for the next three years.

The German children stared in awe at the treasure trove of cake and fresh fruit as the organisers began the introductions. Among their number was a five-year-old who had been accustomed to a life dominated by the sound of air raid sirens and bomb raids. Most alarmingly was the spectacle of eight-year-old Elizabeth Kohlberg, who had no idea where she was and shook in terror at the prospect of being sent to a slaughterhouse.

Protestant and Catholic relief agencies in Germany selected children between the ages of five and fifteen who were brought here in 1946 and 1947, first to Glencree and later to their temporary homes. Five hundred German children were fostered in this way. It was considered that rearing Jewish children would prove too difficult a task in a predominantly Catholic society.

A number of the refugees were orphans, but most had parents who, faced with the consequences of war, could not look after their children. For that reason they were sent all over Ireland. They were obviously badly confused by the way they were sent into involuntary exile, but they found consolation in the warmth of the welcome. Anti-British sentiment did contribute to the generosity of their welcome in certain quarters.

The Scarlet Pimpernel of the Vatican

The late 1930s were a time when Diderot's maxim 'Only one step separates fanaticism from barbarism' was getting a resounding confirmation in the atrocities of Hitler and Mussolini. When the Second World War broke out in Italy, Monsignor Hugh O'Flaherty, better known as the 'scarlet pimpernel' of the Vatican who saved approximately 4,000 Allied prisoners of war from the Germans in Rome, came to prominence.

His wartime exploits, in which he frequently risked life and limb to hide POWs with Roman friends, were chronicled in a book, entitled *The Rome Escape Line*, and a film, *The Scarlet and the Black*, starring Gregory Peck as Monsignor O'Flaherty. He was also the subject of a *This Is Your Life* BBC television programme with Eamonn Andrews in 1963.

Born in Lisrobin, Kiskeam, Co. Cork, O'Flaherty studied for the South African missions with the Jesuits in Limerick before moving to Rome, where he was ordained, in 1925, after being awarded doctorates in divinity, canon law and philosophy. He was given a post in the Vatican diplomatic service, serving, with a pronounced Kerry accent, in Egypt, Haiti, San Domingo and Czechoslovakia, before returning to Rome in 1938. He cut a dashing picture as he stood on the top steps of the basilica in St Peter's Square, standing, according to his biographer, Sam Derry 'six foot two in black soutane, with that utterly Irish rugged face bent over a breviary, glasses glinting on his big nose . . . scanning the square for a familiar figure while murmuring Latin in a Kerry brogue'.

One story gives a great insight into O'Flaherty's remarkable courage and cleverness in outwitting the Nazis. When he was informed that a British soldier faced imminent arrest and execution, he arranged to have him smuggled into Rome under a cartload of cabbages. There the soldier was met by a burly man in black who gazed down from the basilica's left-hand steps and whispered, 'Follow me.' The priest led him to a building known as Collegio Teutonico (the German College), which was outside the Vatican but still on neutral ground. They took refuge in a small bedroom-study, when the priest identified himself: 'Make yourself at home. My name is O'Flaherty, and I live here.' He thought that a British conspirator should be safe in a place filled with German clergy.

The Irish priest delighted in flirting with danger. Once, after he had stored a British general in a secret hideaway, he took the 'guest' to a Papal reception, dressed in Donegal tweeds, and introduced him as an Irish doctor to the German ambassador. He had no qualms about putting his own life at risk if it meant saving the life of another human being. He was particularly adept at bluffing his way past guards while never being so daring that he might jeopardise the Italians who courted death by harbouring soldiers.

His exploits as the *ex officio* head of the underground British organisation in Rome did not go unnoticed and the German ambassador informed him that Lieut-Col Herbert Kappler, the Gestapo chief in Rome, wanted his head. He was told that if he ever strayed outside the Vatican he would be arrested. A trap was laid to draw him to attend to an injured POW in a village 30 miles from Rome, but at the last second one of his moles revealed that it had been set up by Kappler. After the war O'Flaherty often visited Kappler in prison, baptising him when he converted to Catholicism. The German wrote about O'Flaherty from his cell: 'To me he became a fatherly figure.'

The Italian Job

Johnny Carey was also stationed in Italy during the war and played part-time professional soccer for a few clubs under the name 'Cairo'. This led to a number of offers to stay on in Italy as a full-time professional when the guns of war went finally silent. The war robbed the football world of the chance to see Carey in his prime.

On 19 February 1945, Matt Busby's selection as new Manchester United manager was formally announced – just as Busby had been offered the job of assistant manager at Liverpool. Ironically, Busby's playing career had been spent with two of United's biggest rivals, Manchester City and Liverpool.

Busby was born in the tiny mining village of Orbiston, Lanark-shire, in 1909, and was reared in a two-roomed cottage. Loss and hardship were constant features of his early life. He was devastated by the death of his father and all his uncles in the trenches of the First World War and then watched as – one by one – the rest of his immediate family emigrated to the United States in search of a better life.

By the age of 17 the young Busby was set to follow them, and he was waiting for his visa quota number to come up when an attractive alternative offer suddenly came his way: the offer of professional terms with Manchester City. Badly homesick initially, Busby only established himself after an injury to City's regular wing-half. He won his only cap for Scotland in 1933 and the following year he won an FA Cup medal with Manchester City. He was then sold to Liverpool for £8,000 and successfully teamed up in their defence with fellow Scots Tom Bradshaw and Jimmy McDougall.

Busby faced a formidable challenge in 1945. Old Trafford was a tangled heap of wreckage, thanks to direct hits by German bombs in 1941, and United were compelled to accept the hospitality of the old enemy Manchester City, hiring their Maine Road stadium for home matches until May 1949 when, with help from the War Damage Commission, a resurrected Old Trafford finally reopened its gates. Even more problematic, perhaps, was the fact that United were a hefty £15,000 in debt, which meant little or no money for Busby to buy players to replace those who, still on the club's books, were away on military service. Busby immediately signalled a new departure by putting on a tracksuit to join his players in training – a revolutionary move in an era when managers tended to be aloof and to work behind the security blanket of a desk.

His appointment as United's manager followed his stint in the army, where he held the rank of Company Sergeant-Major. He served as a Physical Education instructor. Among his tasks was to lead the British Army team, which included giants of the game such as Joe Mercer, Frank Swift and Tommy Lawton, sent to entertain the British troops in Italy following on from the Allied invasion.

In Bari, Busby met another man with Irish blood in his veins, with whom he would strike up a formidable alliance. Unques-tionably he was one of Matt's best ever signings. Sergeant Jimmy 'Tapper' (given his penchant for his 'it's a man's game' tackles) Murphy was deployed as head of a service sports recreation centre for troops who had defeated Rommel's Afrika Korps in the Western Desert.

Jimmy Murphy's father was from Kilkenny. In the early years of the twentieth century he took the emigrants' ship to seek work in the coalmines. Murphy played most of his football with West Brom, winning 15 Welsh caps before the world found itself at war. Although he was Matt Busby's assistant, he was not officially called assistant manager until 1955. The Busby-Murphy partnership was an instant success, United finishing runners-up in the league four times during their first five seasons.

One of Busby's first decisions was to appoint Johnny Carey as United captain. With his natural leadership qualities, the calm Dubliner was the obvious choice to be the manager's eyes and ears on the pitch.

Their big breakthrough came on 24 April 1948. United's progress to the FA Cup final that year had not been without incident. In the third round, against Aston Villa, they led 5–1 at half-time, but Villa staged an astonishing second-half recovery to score three more goals and threaten to grab the equaliser before the Reds awoke from the slumber to score a late sixth goal to seal victory.

Victories against Liverpool, Charlton Athletic, Preston North End and Derby County saw them poised to win the trophy for the first time in 39 years. However, they faced formidable opponents in the shape of a Blackpool side which featured the combined talents of Stanley Matthews and Stan Mortensen. Both teams attacked from the start and in the 14th minute Blackpool took the lead after Mortensen was felled in the box and Eddie Shimwell scored the resulting penalty. In the 28th minute Jack Rowley equalised. Matthews and Mortensen combined to put Blackpool 2–1 ahead in the 35th minute, Mortensen becoming only the fourth player in history to have scored in every round of the FA Cup. It was not until 20 minutes from the end that United equalised with Rowley's second goal.

After the equaliser United's goalkeeper Jack Crompton pulled off a marvellous save to deny Stan Mortensen and United took the lead for the first time when Stan Pearson unleashed a rocket of a shot from 25 yards which went in via a post. John Anderson scored United's fourth in the 88th minute. The victory was Matt Busby's first silverware as manager, and it marked the beginning of Manchester United's post-war surge to the top.

The United team that day was: Crompton, Carey, Aston,

Anderson, Chilton, Cockburn, Delaney, Morris, Rowley, Pearson, Mitten.

Summertime Reds

That summer Busby led United on a tour to Ireland for games against Shelbourne Select XI and Bohemians. Johnny Carey had almost extended the Irish connection at Old Trafford in 1946 on foot of Ireland's tour of Spain and Portugal. In the opening fixture against Portugal in Lisbon, Ireland were 3–0 down after 30 minutes when the Irish goalkeeper, Cork United's Ned Courtney, went off injured. Defender Con Martin, having occasionally served as an emergency keeper with Drumcondra, took over between the sticks and produced a superlative performance to deny the Portuguese any further goals. In the Spanish match in Madrid Martin played the entire match in goal and against all the odds brought off a series of breathtaking saves to keep a clean sheet. Amazingly, Ireland won 1–0.

Carey was so impressed by Martin's heroics that he recommended him to Matt Busby as the solution to United's goalkeeping problems. Busby responded positively to his suggestion, but as he moved for Martin, Leeds United also intervened. They, however, were offering him terms as a half-back, his preferred position, and Martin opted for Elland Road. A generation later, in 1973, Tommy Docherty brought Con's son, Mick, to United from Bohemians. In 1949 both Carey and Con Martin would link up again in one of the most glorious triumphs in Irish soccer history – the 2–0 defeat of England at Goodison Park. It was the first time England had been beaten on home soil by a foreign team.

The previous September, Carey and Bill Gorman shared the unique experience of playing against England twice within 48 hours, for two different countries. On 30 September they were part of the Eire side that lost 1–0 in Dublin, having been part of the Northern Ireland side that had been humiliated in a 7–2 defeat in Belfast two days previously. Carey won 29 international caps as a United player, captaining the Irish on 19 occasions. In 1952 he led United to their first league title since 1911. The 1950s would see United winning league titles in 1951–52, 1955–56 and 1956–57.

Carey played 344 games for United, scoring 18 goals. He retired in 1953, realising that Roger Byrne, a young full-back, was poised to take his place. United offered him a coaching position but Blackburn Rovers stepped in and offered him a job as manager. After taking Blackburn back to the First Division, he went on to manage Everton for three years. He then took over at Leyton Orient and in his first season took them into Division One for the first time in their history. Following Orient's subsequent relegation he moved to Nottingham Forest in 1963 for five seasons, before ending his managerial career where it began, at Ewood Park.

Carey was not the only Irish player on the United books at the time. Ignatius Feehan joined United in November 1948 from Waterford but had to wait 12 months before making his début, in a 6–0 victory over Huddersfield Town. He played in goal for United on 13 further occasions before moving to Brentford in 1954.

Starmakers

Matt Busby was an astute judge of human character. With the obvious exception of John Giles, he was rarely wrong about players or people. Two of Busby's shrewdest signings were his brace of Irish scouts, Bob Bishop, who scoured the North of Ireland, and Billy Behan, who looked after United's interests in the South. It takes special qualities to recognise a precious talent emerging when watching schoolboy football and to decipher a boy's likely potential when he becomes a man. Whatever that indefinable attribute is, both men had it in abundance.

Bishop was a former shipyard worker who had particular success trawling through youth clubs, so much so that one of his patches became known as 'Belfast Boyland'. His most notable find was, of course, George Best, but his other discoveries, beginning with the late Jackie Scott who joined United in 1952 and went on to represent Northern Ireland in the World Cup finals in 1958, included Sammy McIlroy, David McCreery, Jimmy Nicholl and Norman Whiteside. George Eliot's comment on Dorothea Brooke in *Middlemarch* could apply to Bob Bishop and his contribution to United: 'But the effect of her being on those around her was incalculably diffusive: for the growing good of the world is partly dependent on unhistoric acts; and that things are not so ill with you and me as they might have been, is half owing to the number who lived faithfully a hidden life, and rest in unvisited tombs.'

The appointment of Behan was also an inspired choice. The result of the association was that Behan became a lifelong friend of Sir

Matt Busby, who never failed to express his admiration for the Dublin man's ability to spot talent and for the enormous part he played in the building of teams at Old Trafford. The first two schoolboys he brought to United in the 1940s were Noel McFarlane and Paddy Kennedy. As chief scout Behan's 'finds' included Johnny Carey, John Giles, Liam Whelan, Tony Dunne, Gerry Daly, Paul McGrath and Kevin Moran. His ties with Manchester were strengthened by the fact that he married a Mancunian.

One League of Ireland club was to benefit from the friendship between Busby and Behan. Waterford had a great player in the '50s called Jack Fitzgerald. Behan advised Busby to look at him and the two men went down to Waterford to see him play. During the game Fitzgerald suffered a very bad knee injury from which he never fully recovered. Nonetheless, the Waterford directors treated their two guests like royalty and presented both of them with beautiful 25lb hams. Busby was overwhelmed by their generosity, particularly as, in his eyes, he had done nothing to deserve it. As he left for home Busby told Behan to inform him of any way he could repay their courtesy.

Some time later Behan received a phone call from one of Waterford's directors seeking his advice on whom the club might appoint as a player-manager. Behan suggested that they approach Matt Busby. Hearing of their predicament, Busby suggested that they take one of his players, Eddie McIlvenny – a star of one of the biggest upsets in international football on 28 June 1950 in the first-round match in the World Cup when the USA beat England 1–0. When the result came in, newspaper editors frantically rang their agencies to double-check there was no mistake. The England team had travelled to the tiny stadium and bumpy pitch in Belo Horizonte to face the ill-assorted team of multinational immigrants that constituted the American side wondering how much their winning margin would be. In spite of the wizardry of Tom Finney and the persistent prompting of their captain Billy Wright, England could not force a goal.

Although Busby could have sought a transfer fee for the player from another English club, he allowed McIlvenny to move to Ireland without seeking a penny. The American international led Waterford to years of success.

Coincidentally, both Bishop and Behan took retirement in 1987. Bishop died in 1990, at the age of 90, and Behan passed on to his eternal reward the following year, aged 80.

In the Name of The Father

Billy Behan's son Terry is in the business of beauty. In his office at Oriflame Cosmetic Manufacturers in Sandyford Industrial Estate, Terry has a rich tapestry of memories about his father.

At that time managers were a bit particular about who they signed. You almost needed a character reference to be signed to a big club. That's why, in the early years especially, the scout was so important.

My earliest memories as a child are of Saturday evenings at 5 p.m. when there was never a sound as we listened to the soccer results on BBC radio. My father had a large family, with eight sons, and supplemented his income by working for a bookmaker, so my mother wrote down the results for him. Every Sunday we went off to matches to watch young players. We always finished up in Cabra at Liam Whelan's family home, and that's why the families were so close. I was seven at the time of the Munich air crash and I can still remember the devastation and my mother almost breaking down with emotion.

One Sunday stands out for me. We went to see a young player in Bushy Park. My father wouldn't tell me who it was and asked me to find out for myself. At various stages in the match I guessed a number until I finally gave up. He told me it was number nine, and only then did I see the special qualities he had and appreciate that he had a lot of potential. It was Don Givens.

Did Billy always get his man?

The one that got away from him was Liam Brady. Dad once said: 'I was sure I had Liam Brady because he was a United fan. I was a friend of the family and his brother played for me at Drumcondra. I was certain I'd get him, but as his brothers Ray and Paddy were living in London, his family wanted Liam with them, and that's how Arsenal got him.'

My father was certain Ronnie Nolan of Shamrock Rovers would have made it in England, but there was a surplus of talent at Old Trafford in that position at the time. He considered him the best defensive half-back ever in the country.

He was as concerned with those who didn't make it as with those who made it big. He sent Mick Lawlor to Old Trafford but he didn't make it there. When he came back Dad met him at the airport and fixed him up with a job and a club, and, of course, he subsequently went on to become one of the giants of League of Ireland football over a long number of years.

Which of Matt Busby's successors was he closest with?

Tommy Docherty was the only United manager who signed Irish players without ever seeing them play. If my father recommended somebody, that was good enough for him. In fact, when 'the Doc' moved on he tried to persuade Dad to go with him, but he was too much of a United loyalist even to entertain that suggestion.

Chapter Five

The Busby Babes

'At six o'clock, out of pure curiosity, I turned on my television set. As the news came on, the screen seemed to go black. The normally urbane voice of the announcer seemed to turn into a sledge-hammer. My eyes went deathly cold and I sat listening with a frozen brain to that cruel and shocking list of casualties that was now to give the word Munich an even sadder meaning than it had acquired on a day before the war, after a British Prime Minister had come home to London waving a pitiful piece of paper and most of us knew that new calamities of war were inevitable.'

H.E. Bates captured the spirit of Manchester in the FA's Year Book of 1958–59 in the immediate aftermath of the Munich air crash. The memory of that incident could never be erased, lingering like an unwelcome visitor, leaving an inheritance of quiet despair.

Irish international John Aldridge, himself a native of Liverpool, contemplated retirement after the Hillsborough disaster in 1989. Munich induced similar feelings.

Among the casualties of this swirling tide of death was a young Irishman, engaged to be married, who had already become one of the finest players of his generation. Liam Whelan is the James Dean of Irish soccer.

Both his brothers, Christy and John, played League of Ireland football. Christy never had any doubt that Liam would make it big.

I knew there was something special about him from the time he was 14. We were very close. I was four years older than him. My father died when I was 11 and I was a father figure to him. The most famous name in schoolboy soccer in Dublin for a good number of years was Jim Kennedy. Whenever Liam played against his side he always said: 'I want two men marking Whelan. If we put him out of the game we'll win the match.'

In what circumstances was Liam signed for United?

Manchester United had a great youth team and their inside-right Johnny Doherty was injured. At that particular time Liam was picked for the Irish youth team but there was another smashing player in the side called Vinny Ryan. Vinny captured more of the media attention than Liam did and all of the talk was about him. I often used to say to my mother that there was something wrong in the world because Liam wasn't being taken up by a big club. Even the League of Ireland fellahs weren't approaching him.

Bert Whalley came over to watch Vinny with Billy Behan for Home Farm AUL against Merrion Rovers. Before half-time Bert said to Billy: 'It's Whelan we want.' [Vinny went on to play for Celtic and later came back to play for Drums.] That was on a Friday night in April. I went home from the match and went to bed. I was asleep when Liam came into the room. At the time we slept in the same bed, so I didn't wonder too much until he told me to get up. I asked him what was wrong and he told me that Manchester United wanted to sign him. My exact words were: 'Well, it's about bloody time.'

I got up and put an overcoat on me. I didn't have a dressing-gown at the time. I was introduced to Billy Behan, and Tom Smith from Home Farm was with him, and they told me that they wanted Liam to go to Manchester. My mother asked me what I thought . . .

A new range of emotions suddenly comes to the fore as he thinks of his mother. The normal flow of speech is abruptly impaired. Pauses appear between this sentences. He speaks with obvious pain at her memory.

> I asked: 'Is it a trial or are you taking him as a full-time professional, cause he's too good a player for a trial?' Billy replied: 'We're signing him immediately.' That was it.

Whelan came to Old Trafford as an 18-year-old in 1953, forsaking his job of four years in Cassidy's in George's Street, and made an immediate impact when replacing John Doherty that year in the FA Youth Cup final against Wolves. He starred in United's 7–1 first-leg victory and scored in both legs. He even had the audacity to score a goal with a back-heel.

Such was his brilliance in a youth tournament in Switzerland, the club received an inquiry from South America about his availability. Matt Busby's response to this offer was: 'He was their type of player – he had all the Brazilian skills. They offered me a blank cheque but I told them that all the money in the Bank of England wouldn't buy him.'

The transition to life in the fast lane brought its own teething problems for the Irish wonderkid, as Christy recalls.

> Liam was very homesick, and while he loved the place he said to me once that he'd love to be able to retire and come back to Ireland. I told him he was wishing his life away.
>
> They used to train every morning until lunch-time and then they were free, which didn't suit Liam because he had nothing to do. On a Monday afternoon they were compelled by the club to go to the golf course in the country because the air in the city was so unhealthy with the smoke from the factories.
>
> Johnny Carey looked after him and told him to hang on to the name Liam for as long as he could because they would call him Billy.

Hard Times

The Ireland that Whelan was leaving behind, where TB was rampant, was the country described in Frank McCourt's 1997 Pulitzer Prize winner *Angela's Ashes*. This book offers an invaluable piece of social analysis. In a sense it is a corrective to the nostalgia of the so-called 'golden era of Irish Catholicism' in the 1950s. The book exposes the harsh reality that in the lanes of Limerick, McCourt's little twin brothers died – not because of an accident, but because the society they were born into did not want them within it. This 'Christian community' hardly wanted the destitute to live within its walls. Probably the most haunting image is when Frank is shocked to discover his mother begging outside the church.

Few scenes expose the dehumanising quality of poverty better than this one. It is impossible not to read this book without getting angry because of the chronic indifference to people in need that is evident on every page. Perhaps it is unfair to judge those in a position to help too harshly. They were people of their time. They believed devoutly in the old certainties, most particularly in the Catholic Church as the one true Church, an unchanging fortress in a chaotic world which sheltered the faithful from the evils of an impure world, giving a detailed prescription for the resolution of old dilemmas and the answers to life's problems. They favoured censorship because it 'prevented the flock from being corrupted'. They cherished the infallibility not only of the Pope, or, as they preferred, 'His Holiness', but of bishops, monsignors, parish priests and curates.

Meanwhile, the McCourt family were forced to live in a slum dwelling. Those damp houses hung between heaven and hell in the ghettoes that welcomed no one, a sore, rather than a silent monument to the cancer of injustice. It was a hard school where the lessons were about life and the knocks hard. It is often said that unlike the British the Irish do not have a class system. That is not true, because we have something much more subtle. In rural Ireland in particular there was a very definite hierarchy which kept everybody in their preordained niche. The only way to break free from your appointed status was to move out.

The shadow of emigration lurked like a vulture hovering over its prey. It was the traditional Irish solution to economic problems. It churned out an assembly line of bodies for the boats to England and America. Emigration was central to the Irish culture. Communities were stripped of their young people in the same way a flock of sheep would demolish a field of fresh grass. It shaped the way people thought and felt, conditioning them to accept the grotesquely abnormal as normal. That was the way it was and that was the way it would always be. Although there were no industries, there was one highly developed export: people.

There were many scenes of families travelling *en bloc* to the train station. Everyone wore their Sunday best. The mother was blind with tears. The father's eyes were dry but his heart was breaking. Men did not betray emotion. It would have been seen as a sign of weakness. The young people leaving leaned out of the window, choking with sadness as they saw their parents for perhaps the last time. Younger brothers and sisters raced after the train, shouting words of parting. Sometimes white handkerchiefs were produced and waved until the train went out of sight. Those handkerchiefs gave a ritual, almost sacramental solemnity to the goodbyes. Their presence was a symbol of defeat, a damning indictment of an economy unable to provide for its brightest and most talented.

Hundreds of young and not so young people left every year. The collective tale of woe concealed thousands of individual nightmares. This was most keenly felt at Christmas, when elderly parents were melancholy, pessimistic and moody. In a peculiar way they looked forward to the season of goodwill and yet dreaded it. They were impatient for the magic that never came for them but that all the preparations promised. Christmas was above all a time to be lonely. In their microcosm lay rural Ireland's universality. They remembered their families scattered all over the world: Manchester, Australia, America and Canada. While their children felt exile, homesickness and longing and hoped for returns that would never materialise, they were trapped in a prison of memories. Their pain was the piercing grief of never being able to return to the way things used to be. Like many elderly people in rural Ireland who lived alone, their loneliness became more intense and shrill with each passing Christmas, at times ascending to a chilling crescendo. Every year their longing for warmth and affection became more desperate. They were further silent victims of a vast and concealed cancer of loneliness, an emotional holocaust. Christmas was little more than a painful reminder of missed chances for lasting happiness.

Young people wanted to stay in the country they loved but had no way of making a living. They wanted to be close to family and friends but they had no other choice but to leave. Many had good skills. Some had excellent examination results. Yet the piece of paper that was most important was the ticket to Manchester or America.

And yet the people were in many ways very sophisticated, as was evident in the way they used language. It took real skill to disassemble the easy platitudes and decipher their real meaning. Speaking about a dead priest in rural Ireland, for example, was an art form which a PhD student in psycholinguistics would have found practically impossible. 'He was careful with money' meant that he was a reincarnation of Scrooge. On the other hand, 'Sure he had no interest in money' said that he had allowed the Church and school to fall into rack and ruin. Worse still was 'God bless him, the poor man put a lot of work into his sermons'. This was a dead giveaway. These sermons went on and on like a transatlantic ocean liner. The greatest depth of feeling was evident in an apparently casual remark. 'He didn't suffer fools gladly' revealed that nobody but nobody could get on with him. The poor priest just could not win.

Life was not all fun and games in Manchester either. Liam Whelan came to Manchester when there was something of an economic slump. Under the headline 'Where men run to find a job', *The Manchester Guardian* reported:

> When it is recollected that Great Britain has absorbed millions of workers into her defence forces and has millions more employed on rearmament work, that there is widespread unemployment in the British automobile industry and that there has been only partial recovery in the British textile industry, furniture trades and clothing trades, the unemployment among workers in the productive industries is relatively very much greater than here.

However, unemployment was only 4.4 per cent. Meanwhile in Ireland, the rate of unemployment was twice that figure.

My Brother's Keeper

Whelan was not the only Irish international at Old Trafford who would merit the sobriquet 'Busby Babe' – though Busby himself hated the term. Jackie Blanchflower made his début at Liverpool in November 1951, although he did not establish himself as a regular until the 1953–54 season. He had signed for United in 1950, playing his first game in a friendly at Kilmarnock. His first league game did not come until the following year, however, when he lined up at right-half. Like Johnny Carey, he played in a variety of positions for the club: centre-half, inside-left, wing-half, inside-right and centre-forward. He also acted as substitute goalkeeper.

In 1957 United were poised to become the first club to win the double since Aston Villa in 1897. It was Villa who stood in their way in the FA Cup final. The game was marred by controversy following a sixth-minute injury to United keeper Ray Wood, who was charged so heavily by Villa's outside-left Peter McParland that he broke his jaw and was forced to leave the pitch. He subsequently returned to play on the wing but was nothing more than a passenger. Jackie Blanchflower was delegated to be the emergency goalkeeper, with Duncan Edwards deputising for Blanchflower in the centre of defence. The Irishman performed heroics in goal and kept Villa at bay for over an hour. Two goals from McParland midway through the second half effectively sealed the game for Villa, though, despite Tommy Taylor's late consolation goal for United.

Notwithstanding losing out on the double, United's young side were apparently on the threshold of greatness. With time on their side it seemed as if further honours were inevitable, particularly as United had reached the semi-finals of the European Cup a few months previously. Although they had lost out to Real Madrid, Matt Busby had been bullish enough to remark: 'The only difference between us and Real Madrid was in their experience, and we shall soon acquire that.'

Initially it was as a creative inside-forward that Blanchflower established himself. He scored 24 goals over two seasons and picked up a league medal in 1955–56. Having the luxury of a number of forwards, Matt Busby then chiefly deployed him as a centre-half, where he battled for selection with Mark Jones. Although he lacked a bit of pace he was known to his teammates as 'Twiggy'. His strengths were his footballing intelligence, his quality in the air and a sure touch with either foot.

Blanchflower was the brother of the legendary Danny, who led Spurs to the double. He played for Northern Ireland in the company of Danny, winning 12 caps. Jackie not only shared Danny's bloodline, he also shared some of his wit. This Blanchflower trait was most in evidence before the 1961 FA Cup final as Danny introduced the Spurs side to the Duchess of Kent. She said to him: 'The other team [Leicester] have their names on their tracksuits.' The Irishman quipped immediately: 'Yes, but we know each other.'

The Last Line of Defence

In December 1957 Matt Busby raised more than a few eyebrows when he added to the Irish contingent at Old Trafford by buying Harry Gregg from Doncaster Rovers for £23,500 – a record at the time for a goalkeeper. Christmas came early for Gregg when he made his début for United in a 4–0 victory over Leicester City. Earlier Gregg had played for Dundalk, Linfield and Coleraine. He succeeded Ray Wood in the United goal and went on to make 247 appearances for the club over the next nine seasons.

Gregg was already a Northern Ireland international when he arrived at Old Trafford and went on to win a total of 25 caps. 1958 saw Gregg not only consolidating his place as number-one goalkeeper at Old Trafford but also becoming a major player on the international stage. His performances were one of the main reasons why Northern Ireland secured a place in the quarter-finals of the World Cup in their first appearance at the finals. Gregg was voted top goalie in the tournament. He was also embroiled that year in one of the most controversial goals ever scored in an FA Cup final, when in the 55th minute Nat Lofthouse bundled him over the line for Bolton Wanderers' second goal.

United began their European Cup campaign for the 1957–58 season in Dublin's Dalymount Park on 25 September against Shamrock Rovers, Rovers becoming the first Irish club to compete in the competition. When the draw was made in Zurich, Matt Busby turned around to the Rovers chairman and said: 'You've just got a licence to print money.' United won 6–0 in front of a 46,000 crowd with Liam Whelan scoring two goals. The result flattered United, as four of their goals came in the final 20 minutes. However, the Hoops salvaged some pride with a narrow 3–2 defeat in the second leg at Old Trafford, thanks in no small part to an outstanding performance by Paddy Coad.

In February 1958 the Red Devils were the reigning league champions and the team of all the talents. They were also riding high on the Continent and reached the quarter-final stage of the European Cup competition. The Busby Babes were at their peak.

They went to Highbury on a chilly afternoon seeking two league points. At half-time they looked to be well on the way with a comfortable 3–0 lead, thanks to goals from Duncan Edwards, Bobby Charlton and Tommy Taylor. In the 60th minute, however, David Herd pulled one back for Arsenal and, incredibly, two and a half minutes later they were level following two goals from Jimmy Bloomfield. This transformation would have shellshocked most teams, but the Busby Babes were not for turning and gradually took control of the game. United struck back with goals from Dennis Viollet and Tommy Taylor from a difficult angle. Finally Derek

Tapscott scored Arsenal's fourth. The 5–4 scoreline was an eloquent testimony to the attacking policy of the '50s and provides in some respects the most worthy tribute to the Busby Babes. Those memories are warm and comforting, like the touch of a familiar friend.

Paradise Lost

Later that week the Reds went out to Yugoslavia for the second leg of their European Cup encounter with Red Star Belgrade. In another thriller United drew 3–3 and qualified for the semi-finals of the competition on a 5–4 aggregate.

Then tragedy swooped, like a hawk flying down from the sky, a fearsome beast, ferocious as it ripped and shred and tore, attacking all it saw. Later, people would be struck by the speed at which dreams can be shattered and how close the veil is between life and death. The squad was flying back to Manchester on 6 February when their plane landed at Munich for refuelling. During a third attempt at a take-off the aircraft crashed. Twenty-three people on board were killed.

The crash took the lives of eight United players (five of whom had played in the 3–3 draw the previous day), eight journalists, three United officials, two members of the aircrew (one the co-pilot) and two other passengers – 23 of the 43 who had set out on the flight. The eight United players who died were: Roger Byrne (left-back), Geoff Bent (reserve left-back), Eddie Colman (right-half), Mark Jones (centre-half), Duncan Edwards (left-half), David Pegg (outside-left), Tommy Taylor (centre-forward) and Liam Whelan (inside-right).

The lucky member of the United squad was Welsh international utility forward Colin Webster. He had been due to make the trip to Yugoslavia but owing to a severe bout of flu had had to forego the journey.

The FAI's Yearbook of 1958–59 paid a worthy tribute to their biggest star, Liam Whelan: 'We shall miss the cheerful smile and cheekily efficient football, but we shall not forget him, nor those other Manchester United players so tragically torn from the field on sport's blackest day.'

As always Matt Busby got it spot on: 'The tragedy is that he [Whelan] had the ability to be one of the all-time greats. He had amazing natural ability. I always said that Billy [Liam] would be our di Stefano and Bobby Charlton would be our Ferenc Puskas, the two key men in Real Madrid's great team.'

Whelan was only 22 and was the great hope of Irish soccer in 1958, despite having won just four caps. He had already collected two championship medals and played in an FA Cup final at that stage. He was thoroughly focused, to use the buzz word of our times, and went on to score 52 goals in 96 first-team appearances for the club. He was their top scorer in 1956–57, with 26 goals in 39 games – a significant factor in United's title win that season.

Blood Brothers

Forty years on, the moment when he heard the news of Liam Whelan's death is still fresh in the mind of his brother Christy. With every word the years melt away.

> My mother had this ritual every time Liam was flying somewhere. She always knew exactly when he was due to leave and when he was due to land. Her eyes were always on the clock. Whenever he was due to touch down she would always bless herself and say a prayer of thanks to God for giving Liam a safe journey . . .

His voice is fractured with emotion and although it is scarcely audible his anguish is forever imprinted in my memory. He is reluctant to say too much. The air in the room is heavy with silence as he pauses briefly in his own world. Grief is a private place. A tremendous sense of guilt and self-revulsion sweeps over me at having put this gentle man through this agony.

> I was working for Dublin Corporation and we were on strike that day. I was sitting at home when a family friend came to our house. He thought it was to sympathise, but it was he who broke the news to us. My mother couldn't believe it, wouldn't believe it. She pointed to the clock and said: 'But you're wrong. He's landed by now.'
>
> I rang *The Irish Independent* and at that stage they knew nothing about it. Sometime later we got a call from Jimmy Murphy and he said: 'On behalf of what's left of Old Trafford I want to offer my sincere condolences.' After a while a policeman formally told my mother and all the family the news. Our house was crammed with people that night. After they had all gone home my mother said to me:

'But the police never came. He couldn't be dead.' She couldn't accept it.

Even now Christy cannot comprehend why Liam's radiant eyes had to surrender their sight, nor why his articulate voice had to give away its speech. Justice should not allow the sacrifice of such innocent wealth.

Liam's funeral was a very moving occasion. The family's grief, though intensely personal, was generously shared. The local community, as always in times of adversity, responded magnificently. Everyone rallied around. Every seat in the church was crammed with relatives, neighbours and admirers, all with mournful faces. They had good reason to in this court of human suffering.

Sandy Busby identified the bodies, so none of us had to go over. Liam came home in a closed casket which was never opened. It was a massive funeral. You couldn't see the roads at times. All the way from the airport to the church the roads were lined. The cortège stopped outside Home Farm and the boys from the club placed a wreath on the coffin. We almost couldn't get into the church. The taxi-men put 40 taxis at our disposal, and that was typical of the gestures at the time.

We were snowed under with letters from all over the world. To this day, 40 years on, people from Manchester still send money, at the start of February, to my sister to buy flowers and place them on Liam's grave.

Harry Gregg told me that the last words heard on the plane before the crash were Liam's question to Bill Foulkes: 'If we die, I'm ready, are you?' This was a great comfort to my mother.

After the crash the different denominations held their own services. They held the Catholic service in King's Hall in Manchester, the boxing hall. It held 8,000 and another 10,000 waited outside. Two hundred priests celebrated. The priest's sermon was just about Liam and the example he was to British youth because of that remark on the plane.

As a man he never got beyond himself. He loved the people of Cabra and they loved him. He came over once to see me play in a seven-a-side in Killester, a few weeks after playing in the cup final against Aston Villa when he had been picked as the man of the match. Our goalie didn't show up and Liam said: 'I'll go in goal.' I replied: 'Stop messing,' but then I discovered he was serious. Frank Roe was in charge of our team and we talked about it. When I got to the dressing-room I put on the goalkeeper's jersey. Liam was insisting that he play in goal until I told him the fans would be disappointed if he didn't play outfield. So he agreed and we won.

After the match he was due to go on holidays to Kilkenny for two weeks. He asked us when our next match was, and when we said Tuesday he asked would we like him to be there. So he broke up his holidays to be back and was also there for the final. Ourselves and our opponents lined up before the match like a cup final and the national anthem was played. Liam said: 'This is better than a cup final at Wembley.' When the word went around that Liam would be playing, there was a massive crowd, and we won the game.

He was always very good to our family, especially my mother. Every time he went abroad he brought her home a souvenir. We have a glass case full of them at home.

Himself and John Giles would have gone on to be two great forwards for Ireland, but God knows best.

Even now we've still close links with United. Matt Busby called to our house a few times before and after Liam's death. When my mother died in April 1996 one of the club's directors, Les Olive, came over for the funeral and spent the whole day with us.

Terry Behan adds another strand to the story.

Liam Whelan was an extraordinary person. He left Ireland as a very shy boy. Matt Busby told my father: 'He is doing things in training that I can't believe. When that fellah starts to do it in games, which he will eventually, he'll be a class apart. His potential is unbelievable.'

Liam shared digs in Manchester with Bobby Charlton even though he was a few years older than Bobby. They quickly became like brothers. It was a 'First up, best dressed' situation with them, as they even shared their clothes.

When Bobby was 16 he wrote a letter to his mother saying that he wanted to become a Catholic. She was very upset by that and dashed up to Manchester to see Matt. She was furious and said: 'I knew this would happen because this is a Catholic club and you try to influence the boys. I should never have let him come here.' Matt told her to calm down and that there was nobody influencing Bobby. He persuaded her to stay on for a week and judge for herself. When the week was up she came back and said to Matt: 'If my Bobby wants to be what Liam Whelan is, he's welcome.' Busby told my father that that's the greatest compliment he's ever heard paid to anybody. Although Bobby didn't convert to Catholicism, the amount of work he's done for Catholic charities is enormous.

My father often answered the phone calls at Old Trafford. There was a lot of crank calls, including one man who rang every day saying Roger Byrne was still alive in Germany and that he could prove it. Mrs Charlton was also there at the time. She did great work making tea for everybody.

They Died Too Young

Like a flashing sea of rescue cancelling the black night, Harry Gregg exhibited heroism of an extraordinary kind after escaping significant injury. On a number of occasions he returned to the wreckage of the plane to rescue the injured. He first rescued the 20-month-old daughter of Mrs Vera Lukic, wife of the Yugoslavian air attaché in London, who had been given permission to hitch a ride on the charter flight. Then he went back to rescue her mother. Although he thought both Bobby Charlton and Dennis Viollet were dead, he grabbed the two of them by their waistbands and trailed them through the snow.

Thrown clear of the crash, a shoeless Bill Foulkes stumbled back to see whom he could help. It was he who discovered Matt Busby, still strapped in his seat. Clearly badly hurt, Busby was comforted by Foulkes and Gregg, who kept his icy hands warm by rubbing them. After routine treatment in the Rechts der Isar Hospital, Gregg returned home.

Bobby Charlton once said of the great Duncan Edwards: 'If I had to play for my life and could take one man with me, it would be Duncan Edwards.' Although only 21, Edwards had already won 18 England caps in 1958. He fought bravely, clinging on to life for 15 days before finally succumbing to kidney failure. Apart from severe shock, he had suffered chronic kidney damage, broken ribs, a pneumothorax, a broken pelvis and a smashed right thigh. Six days after the crash his condition deteriorated and an artificial kidney was rushed from Freiburg. He was dialysed five times but it was not enough.

Jackie Blanchflower survived, having received the last rites, but never played again. He was unable to leave the Rechts der Isar for three months. His pelvis was fractured, his kidneys had been squashed by the seat belt and every rib was broken, along with both arms and both legs. He tried training again, but he had a bad arm, which had metal gangrene in it. At just 25 his career perished. Likewise, John Berry never played again, and goalkeeper Ray Wood's top-class career was finished in all but name.

There was considerable controversy over the cause of the crash. Two inquiries were conducted by the Germans, which found that the decisive cause of the accident lay in wing icing and that runway slush was a further source. In June 1969, 11 years after the tragedy, the final findings of the British Court of Inquiry, the Fay Report, into the Munich crash were published. The key witness in the inquiry which cleared Captain James Thain from blame for the crash was a German pilot who was at Munich airport on the day of the disaster. Herr Reinhard Meyer said: 'There was nothing like frost or frozen deposit on the wing of the BEA Elizabethan airliner as it lay at the end of the runway. There was melting snow only.'

Murphy's Law

Having being promoted from coach to assistant manager in 1955, it fell to Jimmy Murphy to steady the ship after Munich because the plane crash had left Matt Busby on the brink of death. As manager of Wales Murphy had been on international duty, which meant that he had missed the trip to Belgrade. When he returned to Old Trafford he had no idea what had happened. There was only a skeleton staff on duty, but an unnatural atmosphere seemed to hover in the air. A hysterical secretary greeted him and broke the news. He took a bottle of whisky from a sideboard, sought sanctuary in his own office and wept.

It was Murphy who signed players and imbued all concerned with a will to continue – motivated not by a fear of failure but by the desire to partake in a glory-laden adventure. His steely determination and will to win combined with a natural modesty and plenty of good humour.

His was a remarkable achievement in any circumstances. In this case the word 'remarkable' is barely adequate. Loyalty was his creed, and he turned down lucrative offers to manage English clubs like Arsenal and overseas sides from Juventus to Brazil. Murphy was responsible for nurturing young talent and generated an assembly line of quality players including Duncan Edwards, Bobby Charlton and George Best.

United's first match after the disaster was on 19 February 1958, when they beat Sheffield Wednesday 3–0 in a fifth-round fixture before 60,000 highly charged fans. It was the beginning of a wonderful career for a young Irishman.

Shay Brennan joined United as a 16-year-old in 1953 but did not get the opportunity to shine for five seasons. Despite playing at outside-left instead of his customary full-back position, the 20-year-old made a sensational impact in front of the appreciative Old Trafford audience, scoring two goals in the 3–0 victory. The fact that Brennan was an attacking full-back with excellent ball control made the transition to the unaccustomed position much easier. In those moments, those breaths of time, when sadness and joy share the narrow path of life, hope glowed like a light in darkness.

A further victory over West Brom secured an FA Cup semi-final place against Second Division Fulham. United advanced via a 2–2 draw and a 5–3 victory in the replay. Given the unique circumstances, the FA made a concession to United and allowed them to field two cup-tied players, Stan Crowther (signed from Aston Villa) and Ernie Taylor, a cup medal winner in 1951 and 1953 with Newcastle and Blackpool respectively. The legendary Hungarian Ferenc Puskas offered to play for United but the Football League still operated a ban on foreign players.

Both Bobby Charlton and Bill Foulkes, survivors of the Munich crash, lined up for the Reds in the 1958 FA Cup final against Bolton with the backing of unprecedented popular support, just a few months after the tragedy. Bolton's 2–0 win was secured courtesy of a sterling performance by Nat Lofthouse. Despite the defeat it had been an incredible achievement on the part of Murphy to lead United to Wembley in the most difficult of circumstances.

The 1950s saw the darkest hour in Manchester United's long history, but the 1960s would see its finest. One man was responsible for the dramatic upsurge in United's fortunes, the man Ray Wilkins described as 'The figurehead of figureheads': Matt Busby. As he lay in his hospital bed after Munich, determination and dejection were interspersed. The nurses had ant-like order conquering chaos, bringing swift ease and massaging his nightmare of torn reality. They were a capillary chain of human hands tending his broken body, wedged in pain.

In the hospital, as he searched the hidden places of the mind for the elusive memory of past happiness, he would learn at first hand the bitter truth of Chekhov's observation: 'For the lonely man the desert is everywhere.' At this time loneliness was his roll call. There was nothing in it but to endure and carry on. Each new day broke on the world with its own pain and misery. It was like living life in a revolving door. His was a tale of hope and disappointment, joy and sadness, love and the loss of love, effort and despair, the human condition itself, unfolding before his own eyes. He fought a heroic fight to find the will to continue, with a grim determination to avoid emotional disintegration and to cling on to his sense of self and personal integrity.

Dreams were essential for his emotional survival, elevating his mind above the junk hoarded there. They were a theatre of boundless possibilities and lofty visions, disturbing what was and inventing what was not. With stoic courage he fought back from the brink of death to build a third exceptional side that would beat all-comers in a magnificent fashion and claim two more championships, the FA Cup and the European Cup.

Before Munich the manager and players had been close, but adversity brought them even closer together. Their respective needs took different forms, but, colleagues in suffering, their need for healing and companionship was equally great. In succeeding years their commitment to each other deepened.

Busby's son Sandy put it well: 'This man came and planted a seed in a bombed-out ground, and he watched the seed grow, he loved it and nurtured it, till the branches started growing outwards and upwards. Then the tree was struck by lightning. He started all over again, loving and nurturing it, and the branches grew and grew to the ends of the world.'

Yet in the years after Munich it is probably fairest to regard the manager as still working through a state of bereavement rather than as settling down to face the future. It seemed by no means certain that he was the leader who would eventually take the club to European supremacy.

Chapter Six

The Second Coming

*'Half a million for Remi Moses? You could get the original Moses
and the tablets for that price!'*

— TOMMY DOCHERTY

In the 1960s higher educational standards, greater foreign travel
and the Second Vatican Council opened the windows of change on
Irish society. Ireland was no longer the place it used to be and Irish
culture seemed to have performed a somersault. The old order was
dying to be replaced by a society that was far more fluid,
cosmopolitan and informal. In short, the country was becoming
more like America.

Like all historical shifts, it was ultimately the product of social
and economic factors, but the greatest agent of this social
transformation was unquestionably the emergence of television,
when topics which had hitherto being shrouded in a veil of secrecy
were openly discussed for the first time in Irish society. Television
was blamed for all manner of new social ills, typified in the late
Oliver J. Flanagan's comment: 'There was no sex in Ireland before
television.' Irish people became aware that they had a lot of
catching up to do in many areas. One example of this was Eamon
de Valera's reaction to a visit to France: 'All I can say is that sex in
Ireland is yet in its infancy!'

In the 1960s Irish television viewers tuned in in their thousands
to *Match of the Day* and fell under the spell of the United team of the
Best, Charlton and Law era, culminating in the European Cup win.

A new cultural phenomenon was spawned which has led to thousands of Irish fans making the journey over to Old Trafford to see Manchester United play at home matches. Interest in United was greatly increased by the perpetual flow of Irish players lining up for the club, including a significant number of full-backs.

Find an Irishman

In the 1959–60 season Shay Brennan made the right full-back position his own. Over the next ten years he was a virtual ever-present, only missing out through injury. He was famous for his tackling and his courage. In 1964 FIFA introduced a new law which allowed players to play for a country other than that of their birth, if they were qualified by ancestry or residence to claim citizenship of their adopted country. Irish soccer would never be the same again. Shay Brennan was the first player to declare for Ireland in these circumstances. The Manchester-born full-back played 19 times for Ireland, captaining the side on five occasions.

He was the first in a long line of players to do so. One of the most infamous of this motley crew was QPR defender Terry Mancini. According to folklore, on his Irish début against Poland in 1973 (John Giles's first game as Irish manager), as the anthems were played, Mancini turned around to one of his teammates and said: 'God, the Polish anthem doesn't half go on.' He was abruptly told: 'Shut up. That's the Irish anthem.'

The Irish propensity to attract players in this way also led to a rash of jokes, such as 'FAI stands for Find An Irishman' and 'All you need to qualify to play for Ireland is to drink a pint of Guinness.' The jokes reached a peak when Vinny Jones, or Vinny O'Jones, as the tabloid press christened him, sought to qualify for Ireland. When he came over to Dublin to check for his grandmother's records, the *Daily Star*'s headline was: 'Begorrah! I'm off to pick up my passport now, Jack.'

Vinny went on to play for Wales. According to one mischievous report, he heard of his call-up in the following way:

Mike Smith: 'Hi, Vinny. I'm the manager of Wales and we'd like you to play for us. You do like Wales, Vinny?'

Jones: 'Of course I do. I've seen *Moby Dick* twice!'

Brennan won a European Cup winner's medal and two league championship medals with United. One of the threats to his tenure as United full-back was Scottish international Francis Burns, who made 155 appearances for United between 1967 and 1972. Burns played 36 league matches and took part in seven out of the eight European encounters leading up to the European Cup final in 1968. However, Matt Busby felt that Brennan's experience would be better suited to the task of marking the great Gento when United played the semi-final second leg against Real Madrid at the Bernabeu stadium. The Irishman performed brilliantly and retained his place for the final. In 1981 Burns joined Shamrock Rovers.

After 355 games for United, in 1970 Brennan went on to play League of Ireland football for Waterford, winning two more championship medals in 1972 and 1973 and in October 1973 helping his team to victory in Ireland's inaugural League Cup. Brennan combined brilliantly for both United and Ireland with Tony Dunne.

Dunne won an FAI Cup medal with Shelbourne in April 1960 just before leaving the Dublin club for a mere £5,000. In his days as a junior he played with St Finbarr's and Tara United as a centre-forward. Although he made his début in a 5–3 loss to Burnley that October, it was an injury to his future Republic of Ireland colleague Noel Cantwell, midway through the 1961–62 season, that gave him the opportunity to claim a regular first-team place. He made the most of his break, and after making just three appearances in his first season, the following term he became a first-choice player. Over the next 12 seasons he went on to make over 500 appearances for the club. Dunne won league championship medals in 1964–65 and 1966–67, missing just two games in those seasons. In 1969 he was voted Ireland's Footballer of the Year.

He was once at the heart of a memorable exchange with colleague Bill Foulkes:

Dunne: 'How's the mouth?'

Foulkes (with four stitches in his mouth): 'She's at home with the kids.'

In April 1973 Dunne was one of seven players, including Denis Law, freed by Tommy Docherty. That August he joined Bolton Wanderers and after five years of loyal service, during which he won a Second Division Championship medal, he left for the United States.

Dunne was never the fastest player in the world, as Bill Shankly acknowledged: 'He goes on an overlap at twenty past three and doesn't come back until a quarter to four.' However, he more than compensated for his lack of speed with his tenacity, the accuracy of his passing and the brilliance of his defensive covering. He won his first cap for Ireland at the age of 20 and went on to collect 32 others, captaining his country on four occasions.

Tony's brother, Pat, had two stints with United. The first came in the late '50s when he had trials as a junior. However, they came to nothing and in 1960 he accepted a professional contract with Everton. Following a brief stay at Goodison Park, Dunne returned home to Dublin and went on to win an FAI Cup medal with Shamrock Rovers. In 1964 United, experiencing a mini goalkeeping crisis, bought him from the Hoops for £10,500 and, in another twist of fate, he made his début for the club against Everton at Goodison Park. He went on to play 66 times for United, 13 times in Europe, before departing for Portsmouth in 1967. He won a league medal at Old Trafford, although it was stolen in a burglary at his home in 1992. When he made his début for Ireland against Spain in 1965, he lined up with his brother and United teammate, Tony.

The Cork Noel

In November 1960, United paid West Ham £29,500 for Noel Cantwell, which at the time was a record for a full-back. Cantwell was something of a surprise purchase when he joined United at 28, but his experience was an invaluable asset.

He grew up at the back of the Mardyke in Cork. It is known as 'the golden half-mile' because it produced so many sports stars, such as former Irish rugby internationals Tom Kiernan and Barry McGann. McGann in fact played soccer for Ireland at youth level when the boys in green were one of 24 teams to compete in the UEFA finals. The Irish finished sixth in the tournament. On their way they defeated Holland. It was a major achievement, since the Dutch side included no less than Johan Cruyff.

McGann is one of the great characters in Irish sport, almost as famous for his waistline as for his skills on the pitch. Once, as he ran on to the pitch, he heard a voice saying on the terraces: 'Who's that fellah?'

'That's McGann, the rugby player.'

'Oh, wouldn't you know it by his stomach!'

An even more damning indictment of McGann's bulk was subsequently provided by Tony O'Reilly's quip: 'Twice around Barry McGann and you qualify as a bona fide traveller!'

After emerging as a player of promise with local junior side Western United, Cantwell moved up to League of Ireland club Cork

Athletic before moving to West Ham United in 1952. He became the Hammers' captain and in seven seasons there he made 248 appearances, scoring 11 goals and leading them to the Second Division title in 1957–58. For his achievements he was voted Ireland's Footballer of the Year for 1958–59.

The high point of Cantwell's seven-year career at United was captaining the Reds' FA Cup-winning side in 1963 (winning 3–1 against Leicester City). Because of his innate leadership qualities he was club captain during the 1966–67 title-winning season, although he only played four matches during the campaign. Injuries dogged his United career but he played 144 times for the club over seven seasons. On the pitch he was renowned for his dominance in the air, his precision passing and his tight control. Off the field he was even more famous for his intelligence and the depth of his thought and philosophy about football. During the final years at Old Trafford his main preoccupation was with coaching, where he gained his coaching badge.

There had been speculation that he might have become Matt Busby's successor as manager of the club, but it was not to be. Cantwell created more than a little surprise when he resigned from his position as chairman of the Professional Footballers' Association in 1967 to succeed Jimmy Hill as manager of Coventry. He brought the Sky Blues to their best ever position of sixth in Division One in 1969–70 but was sacked in March 1972, in the wake of a cup defeat at the hands of Hull. He moved to Peterborough in October 1972, taking the club to the Fourth Division Championship in 1973–74, before taking the manager's job with New England Tea Men in the North American Soccer League in 1977.

In addition to winning 36 caps for Ireland, 23 as captain, and amassing an impressive tally of 14 goals, Cantwell also managed his native country in 1967 and 1968. He represented Ireland not only at soccer but also at cricket.

Cantwell succeeded another Irish international, Joseph Carolan, as a United full-back. Carolan was the quiet man of Old Trafford, having joined the club from Home Farm in 1956. He was United's regular left-back for a season and a half before leaving for Second Division Brighton and Hove Albion for £8,000. He won two caps for Ireland.

Maurice Setters was bought from West Bromwich Albion for £30,000 in January 1960 in an attempt to bring stability to United's defence at an important transitional phase in the side's development. He played 193 games for the club and won a cup medal in 1963. He went on to become part of the most glorious chapter of Irish soccer as right-hand man to Jack Charlton.

Players from Northern Ireland were not ignored at Old Trafford either. Belfast-born Ronnie Briggs was one of four keepers United used during the 1960–61 season, although his one appearance saw him picking the ball out of the net six times at Leicester City. He won two caps for Northern Ireland.

Belfast's Sam McMillan was in the right place at the wrong time. The right place was Old Trafford. The wrong time was to be challenging for the number 11 shirt at the same time as Bobby Charlton. In the early 1960s, Charlton played for four seasons as a left-winger. McMillan also deputised as a centre-forward. Although he got few opportunities he acquitted himself creditably, scoring six goals in his 15 games for the club. In 1963 he moved on to Wrexham and later served with Southend United, Chester and Stockport County. His two caps for Northern Ireland were won during his two seasons at Old Trafford.

The Lost Leader

United went into the 1963 cup final as underdogs. The form team were Leicester City, who had finished in fourth place in the First Division. In marked contrast, United had escaped relegation by a whisker. One newspaper even went so far as to describe them as a 'ragged rabble'. Denis Law, who gave a masterful performance throughout, opened the scoring, and David Herd added two further goals to begin a golden era for Busby's newest team.

The United cup-winning side featured one of Ireland's most distinguished internationals, Johnny Giles. The Dubliner had moved to United from Home Farm as a 17-year-old in 1957. Giles has great admiration for the man who discovered him, Billy Behan.

> My own personal memories of the man stretch back to a day when he called at my father's house hoping to convince my parents that a life in professional football was within my grasp and should be encouraged. His standing in the game and his gentlemanly nature were enough to persuade my parents that I could go to Manchester United. He became firm friends with my father from that day onward.

Billy had an instinct about the game which is unusual, especially these days. He could see something in players that many others could not, and the list of big names which he discovered on pitches around Dublin stands as ample testimony to his rare talent-spotting ability. But his most important attribute was his deep passion for the game which brought him to thousands and thousands of matches to see players from schoolboy level upward.

Giles made his league début two years later, in September 1959, in a 5–1 defeat at the hands of Spurs. It was not the auspicious beginning that he might have hoped for and Albert Quixall reclaimed his place for the next game. However, by the end of the season Giles was playing regularly in the first team. In his four seasons at Old Trafford Giles made 99 league appearances, scoring ten goals. He was part of the United team beaten 4–0 by Everton in the Charity Shield in 1963 and was dropped as a consequence. His response was to seek a transfer, a request which was reluctantly accepted.

Giles was always his own man and was not one for taking the easy option. One of the most revealing insights into his character came in the early days of his tenure as manager of the Irish side. He was taking the squad for a training session before a European qualifier against Russia in 1974. In the previous match against Chile, Eoin Hand had scored with a header from a typically pinpoint Giles corner. During the session Hand asked Giles if he wanted him to go up again for the corners in the Russian game. Giles quipped: 'That would be hard from the substitutes' bench, Eoin!' Hand gave way to Liam Brady.

Giles joined Leeds for £37,000 and went on to establish himself as one of the great playmakers of the game. Matt Busby subsequently said that selling Giles was his greatest mistake. Terry Behan is now the closest person to offer Busby's perspective on the transaction.

My father told me there was a lot of misunderstanding between the management of United and Johnny's father about the arrangements when Johnny turned professional. Dad also felt it was a great pity that United played him on the wing instead of in his position as inside-forward. He rated Giles very highly and said that, with di Stefano, he was one of the best passers in the world. He also believed that Ireland did not fully appreciate Giles. Johnny always wanted to play controlled football which was not very popular in Ireland because they sought an 'up and at them' style, but Johnny was too skilful for that.

Given the talent at his disposal, Busby did not initially miss Giles's sublime skills and United embarked upon an orgy of success, winning two more championships and culminating in the European Cup victory in 1968.

In his time at Old Trafford Giles played an important role in helping the young Irish players to settle in. One of the young men who benefited from his largesse was the most famous writer United has produced – with the obvious exception of Eric Cantona.

The Write Stuff

Eamon Dunphy joined United as an apprentice in 1960 at the age of 16. After two years at Old Trafford he signed professional forms but never made it on to the first team, and in August 1965 he moved to Third Division new boys York City. The following January he moved to Millwall for a fee of £8,000, where his career really took off, and he helped the Lions to win promotion to Division Two in his first season with the club. In his seven seasons at the Den he made 274 league appearances, but his Millwall career is also remembered for his classic book *Only A Game?*, a definitive work which chronicled a season in the life of Millwall FC and in the process furnished a fascinating insight into what it is really like to be a footballer outside the top flight, with all its disappointments, humour, insecurities and petty politics. Dunphy subsequently went on to help Charlton to win promotion to Division Two and Reading to win promotion to Division Three before his retirement. Capped 23 times for Ireland, he jokes, 'I won most of them because John Giles didn't turn up!' After a period with Shamrock Rovers he moved into journalism and wrote best-sellers about Irish super group U2, *The Unforgettable Fire*, and Matt Busby, *A Strange Kind of Glory*.

At 10.30 a.m. on a Wednesday morning, Ireland's most controversial sports journalist is the perfect tonic for drooping spirits. Lively, highly intelligent, articulate, his thoughts explode in a torrent of words and my mind races to keep up. He slows down only to puff on his cigarettes. His intense expression is enhanced by his arresting eyes that sparkle, almost flash, as ideas and indignation energise his mind. His comments are distinguished by his conscientious scrutiny of facts and events, his astute evaluation of personalities and his wry discernment, which means that he never resorts to a clutter of common clichés. Dunphy was another of Billy Behan's boys.

> The scout is a mythical figure in football folklore. The character of this myth is said to be blessed with extraordinary powers which enable him to see what others cannot, to identify greatness in embryo amid the bleak frenzy of schoolboy games in Fairview or the Phoenix Park.
>
> The reality of scouting is that most of the best young players are easily spotted, their talents a matter of common knowledge. The scout's job generally consists of keeping in touch with the local scene, informing his cross-channel employers about the talent around and, if possible, trying to establish a relationship with the gifted youngster's parents. Cunning, rather than wisdom, has been the hallmark of the successful soccer scout. To this rule, Billy Behan was the remarkable exception.
>
> The truth is that Billy Behan was the wise football man who could see the qualities that remained invisible to other scouts who stood alongside him on the touchlines of public parks.
>
> They all knew about John Giles, the most prodigious schoolboy player in the history of the Irish game. Billy Behan was alone in discerning greatness in Tony Dunne. Tony was playing League of Ireland football for Shelbourne when Matt Busby heeded the Irish scout's plea to come to Tolka Park and cast a sceptical eye over a player who would have remained forever unfulfilled had Billy Behan not possessed the gift of seeing beyond conventional wisdom. By the time Manchester United won their two championships and the European Cup in the '60s, Tony Dunne was widely acknowledged to be the best full-back in the British game.
>
> Conventional wisdom was never more insistent than on the question of Kevin Moran. Few, if any, believed that the great Gaelic footballer could make a successful transition to professional soccer. Behan was otherwise convinced and, because of his record, was believed at Old Trafford.

To appreciate this great football man's contribution to Irish sport it is necessary only to imagine a game denied the wonderful gifts of the players he discovered, men whose lives were changed as a result of the wisdom he alone possessed.

Billy saw me play for the Irish schoolboys and on his recommendation Jimmy Murphy came over to watch me play – as did Bill Shankly. Liverpool were a Second Division club then and I had to choose between them and United. Naturally I chose United, but it would probably have been better for me to have gone to Liverpool.

Everyone was a United fan then. It wasn't like now. To go to Old Trafford was like going to Hollywood. The team had been tragically killed in the Munich air crash. I was completely in awe of them. They were heroic names, but it wasn't like now when you always see them on TV. We only saw them in cigarette cards or magazines. To me players like Liam Whelan were heroes, although my main hero was George Cummins, an Irish international inside-forward with Luton. As a boy, when I kicked the ball I was George.

I went to United two years after the Munich air crash, and although it was still a big club it was struggling a bit on the field at the time. The club had changed its policy. Whereas in the past United had bred their own players, they were now buying them in. Although they were spending a lot of money, it wasn't really working.

I went on a trial at the club and Matt Busby watched me play the first half of a match, then he left. Luckily I played well in that half. If I hadn't I would have had a very different life.

What was his relationship with Busby?

Matt was a huge man, very imposing, and had an aura about him that was very powerful and real. Everyone from the greatest player on the staff, probably Bobby Charlton at that stage, to the lowest apprentice was aware of Matt Busby's presence when he walked into a dressing-room or on to a training ground. He just had a remarkable aura, an inspiring aura for players. Whatever you were doing, you notched up a gear or two in his presence. That was his greatest gift.

Matt Busby never really got back to himself after Munich. I think most people in the know would agree with that. He came to the training ground occasionally but in the main it was Jimmy Murphy who was in charge, and he had other coaches to help him like Wilf McGuinness. Matt was very much the public face of the club but not on a daily basis. He spent more time in the office.

When you are young, a teenager, you aren't really aware of the bigger picture. It was much later that I came to appreciate Matt's sociological importance – like the whole Catholic thing. Manchester is a very Catholic city that has experienced so much immigration. It has a large Irish and Italian community as well as a big Jewish community. It's the home of a certain kind of Catholicism which is very conservative. Manchester has a strong Catholic tradition and is therefore a very hospitable place for Irish and Catholics. It has a very cosmopolitan background and is a very un-English city, unlike Birmingham or Sheffield. It's got a fascinating ethnic mix.

Before Busby Manchester United wouldn't have had a very definite Catholic identity, but once he became manager it did. It was very significant that his first captain, Johnny Carey, was an Irish Catholic. Matt was a very Catholic man, a regular Catholic. He hung out with Irish Catholic friends and moved within the Irish community. Paddy McGrath, who owned a night-club, was one of his best friends and an Irish Catholic. Matt identified character with Catholicism and with Irishness, and he believed that character was the key to success in professional sport. He was right on that score if not on the Catholic thing. Liam Whelan was a very devout Catholic and there were always a lot of priests in evidence at United matches, and this added a Catholic tinge to the team.

Matt came here to Ireland a lot to relax. He knew when he was getting a young man from Ireland he was getting a player with a certain disposition. He was very fond of that and regarded that as fundamental to their possible success as players. It was hard to think of a great United team without a significant Irish presence. In fact, the closest to this was the Munich team which was made up of virtually all English players, apart from Liam Whelan.

How difficult was it for a teenager to settle into the most famous club in the world?

We were young then. A couple of other guys came over with me, Hughie Curran and Jim Keogh, and we settled in fairly quickly – though neither of them made it. We lived in digs, worked on the groundstaff, had a few quid in our pockets and chased girls. There was a big Irish presence in the club. You would think that we'd be very upset about leaving home, but we were so excited about the challenge it didn't take long to settle in.

John Giles was like a father to me and to the young players who went. I was five years younger than John. He was a great player and a nice man. At the time footballers were paid very poorly in comparison with today. The only chance that a player had of making a killing was if his team got to the FA Cup final and he could flog all his complimentary tickets on the black market. That happened to John in 1963 and he made the mistake of trusting myself and Barry Fry to sell his tickets for him. We were to get a very generous cut. Unfortunately we sold his tickets to a fraudster and ended up without even a penny. We lost him a thousand pounds, which was a year's salary then. John forgave us and refused to let us pay him back. He wasn't in favour with Matt Busby at that time. He was kind of marginalised.

Why were United so popular in Ireland in the 1960s?

Well, it wasn't just Ireland. They were the world's favourite club in the '50s and '60s because of the Munich air crash; the idea of youth being killed in tragic circumstances was a very glamorous and appealing one. John F. Kennedy was a young president and United were a young football team. England was having a renaissance because of the Beatles. Youth, youth, youth was blowing away the conservatism of pre- and post-war times in all areas of life: fashion, music and sport. Nothing epitomised it more than the Manchester United team, and youth was destroyed. A monumental legend was created. Ireland, like the whole world, had an affinity with that.

How difficult was it for Dunphy to turn his back on that legend and move to another club?

> I wasn't able to break into the first team, which was a very good side, and after five years I moved on. I asked for a transfer because I wanted to play in the first team somewhere. Matt Busby said okay. He made sure I went back to York City rather than to Birmingham City so that I wouldn't reappear here to haunt him – which was not a likely scenario, but he wasn't taking any chances!
>
> Matt was ruthless when he had to be in the interests of Manchester United. When John Giles left he didn't go to another First Division club but to Leeds United when they were near the bottom of the Second Division.
>
> Looking back now, my memory of the time is of lovely people and extreme kindness. Although the club was in a bit of a mess when I was there, it was a wonderful way to live, even if, like me, you were failing to make the grade.'

Another young man from Ireland, though, would have more success and become the most radiant star in the football firmament.

Simply the Blessed

In 1961 two 15-year-olds, Eric McMordie and George Best, set sail from Belfast for Liverpool for a two-week trial period with Manchester United. When they got to Manchester they asked a cab driver to take them to Old Trafford. They were stunned when he replied, 'Which Old Trafford?' They had not realised there was also a cricket ground called Old Trafford.

United's scout in Northern Ireland, Bob Bishop, had discovered Best playing schools football. In 1961 he sent a telegram to Matt Busby which said, 'I believe I've found you a genius.' The trip to Manchester was a big cultural shock to Best, not least because it was the first time he ever wore long trousers! His hero was Real Madrid's di Stefano.

Best was unable to join the club as an apprentice pro because of an agreement between the Irish FA and the English FA which was intended to prevent English clubs from poaching the hottest young talent in the North. Under the terms of the deal English clubs who signed such youngsters had to find proper jobs for the boys until they were 17. Best found work as a tea-boy with Manchester Ship Canal Company.

Best married the spirit of his generation with its sense of freedom and optimism. The anthem for the '60s' generation was 'Hope I die before I get old'. Theirs was the generation which saw an unprecedented departure from previous ages. It was in the 1960s that life as we know it today was shaped and moulded. This was the decade of the Rolling Stones, pirate radio, monster peace concerts, flower power and Mary Quant. Hope and idealism were the common currency at a time when AIDS had never been heard of. Nostalgically, everything about the time seems good: the concern for peace, the socially concerned songs of Bob Dylan, Joan Baez and Simon and Garfunkel. Radio Luxembourg ruled the air waves. Their power play, every hour, on the hour, made instant hits of songs such as Les Crane's prayer *Desiderata*. Only the '60s could have produced a character like George Best.

He made his début for United's reserve team in 1962 against West Brom. His immediate opponent was Brom's regular full-back, Welsh international Graham Williams, who was rehabilitating from an injury – a hard man of the game with an imposing physical presence. A year later Best made his full début against West Brom and again his marker was Williams. United won 1–0 and Best earned good reviews for his performance. A few months later he made his début for Northern Ireland against Wales, and again he faced Williams. The Irish won 3–2 with Best having two 'assists'. After the game Williams made a dash for Best in the players' lounge. The débutant was petrified as the Welshman grabbed him roughly by the face and looked him deep in the eye before taking the wind out of Best's sails by saying, 'So that's what your face looks like. I've played against you three times now and all I've seen of you so far is your arse!'

Inevitably, given his skill, Best was a persistent target of the hard men of the game, but such was his speed that he seldom gave them the chance. A recurring feature of United's matches was the attempts to psyche out Best as he took the field. An example of this trend came from former Irish international Terry Mancini, who had a reputation as a 'robust' tackler. His comment to the United star before their duel began was, 'Don't look so worried, George. I'm in a humane mood today. I've put iodine on my studs.'

Best's importance to the United side is revealed in the story of a staff member at Old Trafford who was informed by a colleague:

'I have terrible news for you.'

'What?'

'I'm afraid your wife is having an affair.'

'Is that all? I thought you were going to tell me that George Best was injured.'

Best was not without his disciplinary problems. In 1970 he was suspended for four weeks after an altercation with a referee in which he knocked the ball out of the ref's hand. Characteristically, in his first game back against Northampton in the FA Cup he announced his return with a fanfare, scoring six goals in an 8–2 victory.

From the earliest days, Matt Busby said of him, 'Don't try to change this boy's style. Let him develop naturally. The rest will come in time.' Busby was a man who walked with kings but succeeded in keeping his feet on the ground at the same time.

The noted sociologist Max Weber distinguished between two types of power: traditional and charismatic. The first depends on the trappings of the office. The second, as in Nelson Mandela, rests purely on the aura of the person. As a norm these two elements are separate but very occasionally – and memorably – they coincide. They collided in the person of John F. Kennedy, who moulded a new presidency out of a form of celebrity power.

Matt Busby too had elements of both, as manager of football's most famous club in the august setting of the theatre of dreams but who also represented the forces of change against the serried ranks of crusty resistance. He had a kind of aura about him that made players want to earn his favour, and a completely natural, straight-from-the-heart sense of how to inspire players. He was able to bring the best out of his gifted but sometimes difficult Irish star. Matt's rule was law, the more demanding of obedience because it was given in a soft, kind, reasonable way against which it was impossible to argue. George Best has acknowledged his debt to Sir Matt. 'On the day of Sir Matt's funeral, I could not help but think of the famous words of George Orwell, that some people are born more equal than others.'

Despite his soft outward appearance, when necessary Busby could be as ruthless as the best of them. According to legend, after United won the league in 1965, the United squad decided they should get an across-the-board pay increase of £15 per week. Denis Law was appointed as the players' negotiator. What is often forgotten is that Law was the first United player to win the

European Footballer of the Year award, in 1964. He gave an extra dimension to the side because of his competitive streak. One story told about him goes back to when Newcastle and Northern Ireland goalie Ian McFaul dived full length to hold a long-range shot from Bobby Charlton. The keeper had just gathered the ball when Law bent down to whisper into his ear, 'I'll be here every time.'

Law went to speak to Busby man to man while his colleagues waited with bated breath. They expected a protracted mediation, but Law returned within minutes. To their disappointment he reported that the news was bad, Busby had pleaded poverty and that he was lucky to get five pounds out of him. The only consolation his fellow players could find was that it was better than nothing. At the end of the week the players found that not only had their pay not increased, it had actually decreased. Mustering all the indignation they could manage, the players complained bitterly to their manager. Busby calmly replied, 'Take it up with Denis. When he came to me looking for money, I let him know how tight we are for money just now and persuaded him to accept a wage cut of five pounds a man to help the club out.'

Best had some memorable verbal exchanges with Law. One of the most famous came when the 'Lawman' was complaining about the people from the Inland Revenue:

Law: 'I've had a final demand from the tax people. Eight hundred and fifty frigging quid. But I wrote them a letter.'

Best: 'Saying what?'

Law: 'Saying I couldn't remember borrowing it from them!'

One person who is ideally placed to evaluate Best's contribution is his contemporary at United, Eamon Dunphy.

> George Best knocked around and went to dances with us. He was a nice man then, as he is now. His public image is not right. It's rubbish. George is a gentleman. Although he tries to be Jack the lad sometimes, he's not really. He was very skilful on the training ground but no one was sure how good he would be and if he would be able to mix it in the big league. Some thought he could never do the same audacious things among men. There were seriously conflicting views in the club about it. The thing about George was that he could do in the First Division what kids could do in the street. His genius was that he could translate his ability on the training pitch on to match days. He was deceptively strong and was a sensation

in the First Division. We'd all seen him doing those kind of magic things before – but against bad players. It was a very different thing to do it against the best players in England.

Was there much envy about his success?

There was no jealousy whatsoever. We all admired him, although we did wish it was us. He was what we aspired to be. He was very popular with everybody at the club and we didn't feel jealous because he had the fame, the girls and the money.

What is Dunphy's abiding memory of United's most famous player?

George and I remain good friends. I was talking to him recently and he reminded me of the fact that I was with him the first time he got drunk! The first time ever was when we were playing a youth tournament in Switzerland and he got so drunk that he had to be carried back, and I was one of the pall-bearers. We put him to bed and he didn't wake up for two days! The fact that I was with him on that historic occasion is my claim to fame!

It might be argued that Best was lucky in that he was in the right place at the right time – when Manchester United were bursting at the seams with talent. The counter-argument is that United were lucky to have Best. Best was not the only Irishman to arrive in Manchester in the 1960s whose legacy vacillates between fame and infamy, however.

Don't Look Back in Anger

Many of the musical greats of Manchester are of Irish descent, e.g. Peter Noone of Herman's Hermits who had a string of hits in the 1960s including the number one 'I'm into Something Good', John Maher and Steve Garvey of the Buzzcocks who frequently charted in the 1970s with songs such as 'Ever Fallen in Love', and the entire cast of the Smiths, i.e. Stephen Patrick Morrissey, Johnny Marr, Andy Rourke and Mike Joyce. However, the biggest name of them all is Oasis.

In January 1943 Margaret (Peggy) Sweeney was born, the fourth

Boardroom banter: Ken Doherty meets Alex Ferguson and Martin Edwards in the Old Trafford boardroom, with the Premiership and World Snooker Championship trophies in the background

Cup fever: Graham Turley (second from left, sitting) and Veronica Guerin (third from left) celebrate with Frank Stapleton's family after Manchester United's FA Cup final triumph over Everton

Roscommon Rovers: (left to right) John Dolan, Frank Stapleton, Pierse Sweeney (hidden), Paul McGrath, Brian Guerin, George Bannon, Paddy Joe Burke, Ray Wilkins and Chris O'Gara, as the United stars visit Roscommon

In the name of the father: Terry Behan and Paul McGrath

Mighty Moran: Kevin Moran (second from left, back row), beside coach
Ronnie Nolan, with the UCD team

Gone but not forgotten: The late, great Billy Behan

Best moves: George Best takes on Dermot Earley

The passing of the torch: Frank O'Farrell and Sir Matt Busby at a dinner dance in Dalkey in 1972. Also in the photo are Noel Murray, Paddy Larkin, Frank Mullen, Jimmy Swan, Harry Smith, Jimmy Ennis and Eddie Gibbons

First dinner dance in the Victor Hotel in 1970. Pictured are Jack Crompton and Sir
Matt and Lady Jean Busby, with the Manchester United Supporters Club committee:
(from back) Frank Mullen (secretary), Jimmy Swan, Eddie Gibbons, Des Healy, Paddy
Larkin, Harry Smith, Jimmy Ennis, Bernie Maguire and
Noel Murray (chairman)

Appointment with the Doc: Tommy Docherty with the girls in 1973. Left to right: Kay Watt, Lena Mooney, Kay Gibbons, Eddie Gibbons and Mary Gibbons

Dressed for the occasion: Gerry Daly, Mick Martin, Tommy Kavanagh, Bill Foulkes and Alex Stepney with the committee members at Dalkey in 1974

A giant amongst men: Unveiling the statue of Sir Matt Busby OBE
at Old Trafford in 1997

Pilgrims' progress: Two of the old guard, Billy Gibbons and Sean Bones, at the
United v. Coventry City match in 1996

Foreign shores: Peter Fanagan, Martina Gibbons, Emma Gibbons, Eddie Gibbons,
Mark Gibbons and Willie Doyle, United v. Porto, 1997

of eleven brothers and sisters. The Sweeneys are descendants of the gallowglass warriors who journeyed from Scotland to Ireland in the fourteenth century as mercenaries, chiefly in the service of the O'Donnells. In the early years they settled in the area around Fanad, in Donegal, where they earned their living as warriors for three centuries. In the fifteenth century, family members headed south to fight for the McCarthys of Cork, and they settled there and, later, in nearby Kerry.

Peggy was born into a life of poverty: six girls slept in the one bed and when she made her first Holy Communion, a huge event in the life of a young girl, her parents had to borrow a dress for her from a neighbour. She left school at the age of 13 and took a job in the local grocery-pub-hardware shop. She went to Manchester at the age of 18 but her mother's illness forced her to return after a year and she got a job as a priest's housekeeper. When her mother recovered she went back to Manchester, and two months later, in January 1964, she met her future husband, Tommy Gallagher, who worked on the building sites.

The Gallaghers are the descendants of the O'Gallchobhair sept, who were located in County Donegal. It is a composite name, from *gall*, meaning 'foreign' and *cabhair*, meaning 'help'. The Gallagher motto *Semper paratus pugnare pro patria* ('always ready to fight for my country') may explain some of Liam's more pugnacious antics.

Tommy's Catholic sensibilities were quickly exposed when the first child was born. Peggy wanted to call him Gerard but her husband insisted on calling him after the reigning pope, Pope Paul. Noel was born in 1967 and Liam arrived in 1972.

As children the Gallaghers spent their summers in Mayo. Like many young people at the time they went to Knock on a pilgrimage, lured by promises of sugar sticks and chocolate. They rubbed shoulders with distraught pilgrims praying to give up cigarettes only to be horrified later to discover themselves trying to light a fag with the same match they used to light a candle in the grotto.

Tommy worked as a DJ around the Irish pubs and clubs in Manchester and had a profitable sideline making bootleg tapes of Irish music. He played Gaelic football for Oisins club. It was important for him to be seen to be Irish, so when he acrimoniously parted company with Oisins he decided to form a rival junior football club, St Bernards, to compete against them. His two eldest sons were recruited in this mission and they made their own makeshift pitch in Cringle Fields in Burnage.

Noel was a useful player, although he acquired the nickname 'Brezhnev' after the Russian President famous for his enormous bushy eyebrows. In the circumstances, Liam's nickname, 'The Weetabix kid', was much more mundane. Like his father before him, Paul became a familiar face as a DJ in the Irish clubs – to such an extent that Noel christened him 'a plastic Paddy'. Paul is one of the founders of the Irish Soccer Supporters Club in Manchester.

The Gallagher household was a turbulent and violent one. Such was the discord that in 1984 Peggy and the children moved out. The important thing in life is not to keep bodies together but hearts. The emotional split had taken place many years earlier.

All five original members of Oasis are of Irish stock. Paul McGuigan ('Guigsy'), the bass player, and Tony McCarroll's parents are from Northern Ireland and ('Bonehead') Paul Arthur's family are from Mayo. The band were a footballing mixed marriage: keyboard player 'Bonehead' and Tony McCarroll, the drummer, are both Manchester United fans, whilst the Gallaghers are massive Manchester City supporters.

In fact, a passion for Manchester City is the one thing the three Gallagher brothers have gladly inherited from their father. Anyone who is Irish Catholic in Manchester is expected to support Manchester United, who have always being perceived as the Catholic team and are by a considerable distance the more successful. However, Tommy Gallagher was never one to yield to the tyranny of conformity. As most of his colleagues were fanatical United fans, he decided to support City just to annoy them.

The Greatest Footballer You Never Saw?

Apart from Tony Dunne, Shay Brennan and George Best, another Irishman among the 31 professional playing members of staff at Manchester United during the 1968–69 season was the late Mick Kelly, who died tragically in South Africa in April 1997 at the young age of 47. A few weeks after his death, the Manchester United programme for their last home match of the season against West Ham described Michael: 'An orthodox left winger, he played for the club's A, B and youth teams as well as making a good number of appearances for the Central League side. A contemporary of current staff members Brian Kidd and Jimmy Ryan, he was a member of the United side which defeated Liverpool to win the Lancashire Senior Cup in 1969.'

Although he spent two years at Old Trafford, he never made the breakthrough into the first team. This was a source of great disappointment to Billy Behan, as he confided to his son Terry.

> One of his saddest experiences was that Mick Kelly never made it big at United. He was perhaps the most naturally gifted player he ever saw. He was also a fabulous rugby footballer at Blackrock, who could have been one of the giants of Irish and maybe even world rugby. Although everyone had high hopes when he went to Old Trafford, it was not to be. He came back and made a bit of a splash in the League of Ireland, winning an FAI Cup medal with Bohemians. Dad always thought it was a travesty that he didn't have the dedication to match his phenomenal talent. Otherwise there are no limits to what he might have achieved at United.

Upwardly Mobile

Winning the European Cup was the glittering prize Matt Busby most cherished – not so much for himself, but as a fitting memorial to those who had lost their lives in Munich. After the triumph, Matt was knighted and moved behind the scenes. It was he who recommended his successor.

Wilf McGuinness had been a very talented United player, having appeared in three FA Youth Cup finals and captained the England Youth team. He made his full début for United against Wolves in October 1955 as a mere 16-year-old. Injuries dogged his career, however, and he missed the ill-fated trip to Belgrade in 1958 because he was recuperating from a cartilage operation. A broken leg in December 1959 ended his career at the age of 22. United gave him a job as coach and he went on to coach the English Youth team. During the 1966 World Cup finals he served Alf Ramsey as a training assistant. In April 1969 he created a sensation when he was appointed as Matt Busby's successor, particularly as he was only 31.

The expected success did not follow, largely because the stars of the European Cup-winning side had left their best days behind them and there was an undercurrent of dissent in the dressing-room. McGuinness showed considerable courage in choosing the same match to drop both Denis Law and Bobby Charlton, but in December 1970 he got the worst possible Christmas present – the sack. When told the news he said he would willingly bleed for the club, and he went on to coach in Greece. His record was not that bad – he took United to two League Cup semi-finals, an FA Cup semi-final and two eighth places in the First Division – but it was not enough for a club who considered success as their right. Sir Matt temporarily stepped into the breach but a long-term solution was required to United's managerial problems.

Frankly Speaking

United's only Irish manager was Cork–born Frank O'Farrell. He arrived at Old Trafford as the apparently ideal solution to United's management crisis following Matt Busby's 'second going'. On the surface he was older and more experienced than his immediate predecessor, Wilf McGuinness. In addition he had a proven managerial track record, having steered Torquay from the Fourth to the Third Division and taken Leicester City to the Second Division Championship. The omens seemed favourable when United showed their confidence in their new boss by promoting Matt Busby to the board.

O'Farrell was a graduate of the hallowed West Ham soccer academy of the '50s which produced a succession of managers such as Malcolm Allison, Dave Sexton, Noel Cantwell, Ken Brown and John Bond. O'Farrell's teams would reflect the exciting and attacking football of the best Upton Park tradition.

His West Ham career began in 1948, and he had eight seasons with the club before moving to the then First Division Preston North End in a player exchange which saw Preston's former Manchester United full-back Eddie Lewis moving to Upton Park, making 118 appearances at the club before moving to Southern League club Weymouth as player-manager.

He scored two goals in his nine internationals and played in one of Ireland's most controversial games ever. Brian Moore began one of his short stories in the following way: 'In the beginning was the word, and the word was NO!' This sentence cleverly sums up the experience of those who were brought up to see Catholicism, Irish-style, in a painfully negative way. Sex was never mentioned in public. The so-called 'deed of darkness' was intended simply for the creation of more baby Catholics. This was the time when the Archbishop of Dublin, John Charles McQuaid, had John McGahern dismissed from his teaching post in Clontarf following the publication of his controversial book *The Dark*.

The Catholic ethos of the 1950s even affected the Irish soccer team. When communist Yugoslavia came to Dalymount Park on Wednesday, 19 October 1955, Archbishop McQuaid was so incensed that he instructed all Roman Catholics to boycott the match. Despite his promptings, and demonstrations outside the ground, 22,000 fans attended. Apparently God was on the side of the godless, as Yugoslavia won 4–1. The match was effectively decided by a first-half hat-trick by Milutinovic. Ireland's consolation goal was scored by Middlesbrough's Arthur Fitzsimons. The Irish were captained by Everton's Peter Farrell.

In June 1971 Frank O'Farrell took over at United. Eamon Dunphy has an interesting spin on the Corkman's appointment.

> The club made a lot of errors after Busby retired. They appointed two Catholic managers, McGuinness and O'Farrell, but Matt stayed in the background. He was still there and no one was really sure who was calling the shots. The transition was not handled well. Busby identified character with a Catholic background and it's obvious that in seeking a successor he sought those qualities.

O'Farrell got off to a flyer. By Christmas in his first season United were five points clear of the pack and in the process had served up some very attacking football – but he went on to disprove the validity of the maxim that in any sphere of life, a good start is half the battle. There were plenty of doom-and-gloom merchants who predicted that the bubble would quickly burst, and a series of defeats saw the team sliding down to a mid-table position. It should have been the best of times for O'Farrell. It was the worst of times. His problems were threefold.

Firstly, there was George Best. The Belfast genius had publicly backed O'Farrell's appointment but the romance quickly turned sour. Best's star was waning rapidly, while his tendency to go AWOL was increasing. If his performances on the field were up to scratch, his off-the-field indiscretions would be readily forgiven. The Corkman tried every possible strategy to get the best out of Best. He befriended him, excused him, bullied him, dropped him and, as a last resort, placed him on the transfer list.

His second problem emerged with crystal clarity at that juncture. He discovered that Best and Busby had had a covert meeting in a desperate attempt to sort out their problems. Best's name was removed from the list and in the process O'Farrell's authority was destroyed. Had the Best problem been resolved in the early days while O'Farrell still enjoyed the confidence of the playing and backroom staff it might have been different, but this was a bridge too far. When he finally grasped the nettle, the board refused to give him the support he needed. Inevitably the disharmony spilled over into the dressing-room.

The third problem was his failure in the transfer market, although he did pull off a considerable coup by landing Scottish player of the year Martin Buchan from Aberdeen for a mere £125,000 – surely one of the bargains of the 1970s. The classy central defender exerted the type of influence on the pitch that Bryan Robson would command ten years later. However, O'Farrell's main priority was to find a striker while he did nothing to plug the other gaping holes in the United side, such as in midfield.

He splashed out £200,000 to Third Division Bournemouth for Ted McDougall in the hope that his goals would haul the Red Devils away from the relegation zone. The future Scottish international had impressive credentials, having scored 103 goals in 146 games for Bournemouth. Sadly for both McDougall and his manager, things did not work out according to plan as he scored only five goals in his eighteen appearances for the club. Another disappointing purchase, this time from Manchester City, was Welsh international striker Wyn ('Wyn the Leap') Davies, then in the autumn of his career, who managed just four goals in his sixteen games for United.

O'Farrell also forked out £200,000 for English international Ian Storey-Moore, who had finished top scorer for Nottingham Forest in five of the previous six seasons. Moore was a big, powerful winger with the flair to whip a crowd up to a frenzy and win a game out of nothing. United did well to secure his services because Derby County were convinced they had signed him – to the extent that they paraded him before their fans at the Baseball Ground. Moore, though, had not actually signed on the dotted line and the Red Devils snatched him from under Derby's noses. Although he scored in his first three games for United, a proliferation of injuries, culminating in an accident to his ankle in the gym, meant that Moore never made the expected impact at Old Trafford and he was forced to retire prematurely. With a fit Moore firing on all cylinders, things might have been different for the club and the manager.

Among O'Farrell's other signings was Trevor Anderson, who joined United from Portadown for £20,000 in 1972. In his most optimistic moments O'Farrell may have seen him as a replacement for George Best. His stay at United was less than a resounding success, although he won six of his twenty two caps for Northern Ireland during his time at Old Trafford. After eighteen appearances for the club, which included five as substitute, and three goals, Tommy Docherty sold him to Swindon Town in November 1974. Anderson's star rose again in this new environment. He is probably best remembered for scoring a hat-trick of penalties for Swindon in a league fixture in 1976.

A 5–0 defeat at Crystal Palace on 16 December 1972 was probably the final nail, perhaps five nails, in O'Farrell's coffin. O'Farrell's problems were compounded by the fact that at the time Manchester City were riding high and Malcolm 'Big Mal' Allison was the media's darling. Moreover, Rodney Marsh had eclipsed George Best in the flair-on-the-pitch stakes.

The Irishman was sacked with three and a half years of his contract to run and replaced by Tommy Docherty, who had just guided Scotland through the qualifying rounds for the 1974 World Cup finals. In typical Doc style he boasted that United manager was the 'best job in football'. In addition he said he was prepared 'to walk from Scotland to Old Trafford for the job'. One wag was heard to mutter that that was probably because the Scottish FA was too mean to give him the expenses! The Doc's salary was £15,000 a year, twice as much as he earned for the Scottish job.

The popular perception was that O'Farrell was too remote and used his office as a retreat. Had he been given the time and authority that Alex Ferguson received it might have been different. He was the victim of what Freudians call a 'displacement activity'. The board of directors who despaired of United's sliding fortunes sought a soft target, O'Farrell, when the real problem remained untouched – ageing star players whose best days were behind them.

Dennis Law said of him, 'Mr O'Farrell came as a stranger and went as a stranger.' After leaving United he managed Torquay and later went to the United Arab Emirates as a coach. At Old Trafford O'Farrell was to discover at first hand that nothing recedes like success.

Tommy and Gerry

After his appointment as United manager Tommy Docherty went on a spending spree, forking out £500,000 for four Scots in just three weeks. First he went to Arsenal and signed George Graham for £125,000. Football's bellybutton is liberally sprinkled with bootroom banter, boardroom battles, thrilling tricksters and walls of waffle. In this environment some comments from football personalities are meant to amuse, and others are meant to enlighten. Many of the funniest football quotations fall into the second category! Few managers prove more conclusively than Docherty that for wit, originality and generally great laughs, it really is 'a funny old game'.

Classic 'Docisms' include the following: 'He [Aston Villa chairman Doug Ellis] said he was right behind me, so I told him I'd rather have him in front where I could see him'; 'The ideal board of directors should be made up of three men – two dead and one dying'; 'He [Ray Wilkins] can't run, he can't tackle and he can't head the ball'; 'The only time he goes forward is to toss the coin'; 'He's [fellow coach] not so much a coach as a hearse'; 'There's a hell of a lot of politics in football. I don't think Henry Kissinger would have lasted 48 hours at Old Trafford'; 'Robert Maxwell has just bought Brighton and Hove Albion, and he's furious to find it is only one club'; 'They serve a drink in Glasgow called the Souness – one half and you're off'; 'Preston? They're one of my old clubs. But then most of them are. I've had more clubs than Jack Nicklaus'; 'Some teams are so negative they should be sponsored by Kodak'. However, the most bizarre quotation that ever came from Docherty's lips was surely his response to the signing of Graham: 'George is the Gunther Nezter of British football.'

Then the Doc went to Shrewsbury and signed Jim Holton (now sadly deceased) for £80,000. Although a huge favourite with the fans, Holton was not exactly synonymous with skill. Docherty would subsequently say of him, 'We put bells on a football so he would know where it was. We had complaints from morris dancers saying he was kicking them all over the place.' The quartet was completed by the signing of Alex Forsyth from Partick Thistle for £100,000 and Lou Macari from Celtic for £200,000.

Out went George Best after he failed to show up for training – which was not an unusual occurrence, but this time it was the last straw. He went on to play for a string of clubs in America, England, Scotland and Ireland – the most memorable of which was probably a 42 league-match run with Fulham where he linked up with a footballing soulmate and fellow artist, Rodney Marsh.

Then, as it appeared that Docherty wanted to turn Old Trafford into an all-Scottish enclave, he swooped for two of Ireland's hottest rising stars, Gerry Daly and Mick Martin from Bohemians. Martin was already an Irish international and the transfer fee of £20,000, at the time a record for a League of Ireland club, reflected his status. His pedigree was confirmed when on 3 July that year he played in a Shamrock Rovers All-Ireland XI chosen by Johnny Giles and Derek Dougan against World Cup-holders Brazil. With Dougan and Terry Conroy, Martin scored one of the Irish goals in a 4-3 defeat.

In spite of winning 51 caps for Ireland, Martin never really made the grade at Old Trafford, making forty three appearances, seven as a substitute, and scoring two goals in his three seasons with the club. He went on to play for West Bromwich Albion, Newcastle United, Vancouver Whitecaps, Cardiff City, Peterborough United, Rotherham United and Preston North End.

Daly joined United from Bohemians for £12,000 in 1973. His United début came the same year on his 19th birthday against Bari in the Anglo–Italian tournament. That year also saw Daly making his international début – an occasion made memorable by the intervention of his teammate Ray Treacy.

> I rang up Gerry and pretended to be the well-known Manchester journalist David Meek. I asked him all the type of stuff he was famous for and told him a photographer would be around to the hotel to take some pictures. We borrowed a camera from doctor Bob O'Driscoll, and bribed one of the hotel staff to act the part of the photographer and line him up all around the hotel and finally in the foyer. We made him do all kinds of poses with his gear, such as posing with his foot on the ball. We even got him to wear his crucifix outside his shirt. We then reminded Gerry to be sure to get his fee from Meek.

Daly's arrival coincided with a sharp decline in United's fortunes. They managed only ten wins all season and were relegated to the Second Division for the first time since 1937. Daly hit a hat-trick in United's opening home fixture in Division Two against Millwall. He scored eight further goals that season as United swept the boards in the lower division and easily won promotion.

The following season looked set to end in triumph when United faced Second Division Southampton in the FA Cup final. As had been the case in 1973 when the mighty Leeds were shocked 1–0 by Second Division Sunderland, however, United lost by a single goal. In tears after the match, Daly was consoled by the man who had signed him for United, Tommy Docherty. However, the United manager and Daly fell out and the Irishman was quickly on his way to Derby County, managed by Colin Murphy, for £180,000, which was then a record for an Irish player. Consequently Daly missed out on United's triumph over Liverpool in the 1977 cup final, but at Derby he enhanced his growing reputation as one of the most creative players in the British game. Ironically he was reunited with Docherty the following season after the Doc was sacked by United following the scandal surrounding his affair with Mary Brown, the wife of United's physio. Daly was back where he started and his true talent did not blossom as it should have, despite his exceptional skills.

Daly was one of the key players in the Ireland side under John Giles and Eoin Hand which 'nearly qualified' for all the major championships during these years. He played in a couple of the early matches under Jack Charlton but missed out on the 'glory days' under Jack. After his playing days were over Daly went into non-league football management, becoming player-manager with Telford United of the Vauxhall Conference.

In his book *United to Win*, Ron Atkinson gives an amusing insight into how personality clashes between a player and a manager can end a player's career at a club. In his pre-United days Atkinson had succeeded John Giles as manager of West Brom. One of the players he inherited was Irish international Paddy Mulligan, who had given great service to the club but who was then in the autumn of his career. Big Ron took an instant dislike to the Irishman's verbosity and Mulligan found himself in the reserves. Atkinson's assistant, Colin Addison, suggested the manager should meet Mulligan in an effort to lift his spirits. When Paddy arrived in the office he took the initiative and said, 'Boss, I don't think you like me.' True to form, Atkinson did not mince his words and replied, 'Paddy I can't stand you!' Mulligan responded, 'Can I take it, then, that I'll be going at the end of the season?' 'You can bet money on it!' Atkinson countered. After Atkinson left the office, Colin Addison commented, 'Thanks, Ron. I only brought him in so that you could give him a bit of a confidence-booster.'

No player suffered more from 'the slings and arrows of outrageous fortune' in the form of a manager's whims than Gerry

Daly, although the tragic death of his baby son helped put the vagaries of his career in its proper perspective.

A Ray of Hope

Having signed Mick Martin and Gerry Daly from Bohemians, Tommy Docherty also moved in to sign two players from Shelbourne in the same year. The son of former Drumcondra star Derek O'Brien, Ray O'Brien joined United from Shelbourne for £40,000 after the Dublin team lost the FAI Cup final to Cork Hibernians in May 1973. O'Brien was an accomplished left-back like his brothers Derek and Fran, who lined out for Philadelphia Fury and Boston United respectively in the 1970s. However, Ray never made the breakthrough into the United first team and after only ten months he moved to Notts County for what proved to be a bargain buy at £45,000. In his nine seasons with the club he made 323 league appearances and in 1979–80 he ended the season as their top scorer with ten goals, the first full-back in the club's history to achieve that distinction. The following season he was part of the County side that won promotion to Division One for the first time in 55 years. O'Brien won four international caps.

Paddy Roche joined United from Shelbourne for £15,000 in October 1973. At first he was understudy to Alex Stepney, before Dave Sexton gave him the number one jersey. While he turned in some brilliant displays, notably in a league match against Arsenal, his performances lacked consistency and he lost his place to Gary Bailey. In 1982 he moved to Brentford and two seasons later joined Halifax, where he went on to make 184 appearances.

Our Friends in the North

The Doc, though, had a more benign influence on the careers of a number of Northern Irish internationals. After three seasons with Everton and four with Nottingham Forest, Tommy Jackson joined United on a free transfer in the close season of 1975. Initially Tommy Docherty saw him as the captain of the reserves who would lend his experience to help United's youngsters develop their talent. However, such were Jackson's performances in pre-season that the United manager got other ideas and decided to deploy the Northern Ireland international in the heart of United's first team.

However, Gordon Hill's arrival from Millwall the following November led to a restructuring of the United midfield. At Millwall Hill had earned the nickname 'Merlin' for his sorcery on the wing. He was less assured, though, of his defensive duties, Martin Buchan once boxing his ears during a match for his recklessness at the back. Hill's flair, however, was more to the Doc's liking than Jackson's dependability, and the Northern Irish international found himself surplus to requirements. After 23 games with United, he was given a free transfer before leaving the League.

Tommy Docherty paid Spurs £30,000 for Chris McGrath. He made 15 full appearances for the club and 19 as substitute, scoring one goal. Although he was very skilful on the ball, he had a tendency to run into cul-de-sacs. After four seasons at Old Trafford he joined Tulsa Roughnecks in America. The winger won 21 caps for Northern Ireland.

Like Liverpool's David Fairclough, Belfast-born David McCreery earned the nickname 'Supersub' during his United career. He made 57 full appearances for the Reds and 51 as substitute. He was also known as 'Roadrunner' because of his incredible workrate.

The high point of his time with United came in 1977 when he replaced Gordon Hill in the Red Devils' 2–1 FA Cup final victory over Liverpool. The previous year he had also replaced Hill in United's cup final defeat at the hands of Southampton. In August 1979 Tommy Docherty swooped to take him to QPR for £200,000. He went on to play for Tulsa Roughnecks, Newcastle United and Hearts and to manage Carlisle United and Hartlepool United. He won 67 Northern Ireland caps, most of them partnering another United midfield star.

Supermac

Sammy McIlroy joined United as an apprentice in 1969. The 17-year-old announced his arrival in the Reds' first team in bold print in 1971 with a sizzling début in which he scored one goal and got two 'assists' in United's derby fixture at Maine Road which finished in a 3–3 draw. It would be two years before he could consider himself a regular with the club, but he was an ever-present in the United side which captured the Second Division Championship in 1974–75.

He is perhaps best remembered for his two losing FA Cup final appearances rather than for his winning one in United's 2–1 triumph over Liverpool in 1977. The first defeat came against

Southampton the previous year when he almost forced a draw for United with a header that crashed off the woodwork.

In 1979 Arsenal, with Liam Brady giving a 'man of the match' performance, were cruising to a 2–0 victory with just five minutes to go. The Arsenal manager, former Northern Ireland international Terry Neill, had even decided to take the luxury of replacing his midfielder David Price with substitute Steve Walford, apparently just to give the youngster a taste of the glory. Then Gordon McQueen scrambled a goal for United. Almost immediately McIlroy made a jinking run through the crowded defence before unleashing a bending shot past his Northern Irish colleague Pat Jennings.

The Arsenal players looked totally baffled and dejected. Wembley suddenly seemed transformed into a sea of Manchester red and white. Somehow, though, Liam Brady found a last drop of energy to set up a movement which led to Alan Sunderland sensationally scoring a last-gasp winner. McIlroy captured the mood of the United players: 'It was like picking eight draws and then finding the pools coupon still in your pocket.'

The arrival of Bryan Robson at Old Trafford in 1981 effectively signalled the end of McIlroy's United career and he joined Stoke City for £350,000. He went on to play for Manchester City, Bury and Preston before finding success as a manager of several non-league clubs, striking the jackpot with Macclesfield Town whom he led into Division Three in August 1997.

He won 88 caps and was an integral part of the most glorious chapter in Northern Ireland's soccer history – which in part explains why he was awarded the MBE – as they went on to World Cup glory in Spain in 1982 and Mexico in 1986. Yet another United player was part of this success story.

Literary Centre Circles

Canadian-born Jimmy Nicholl moved with his family to Belfast in 1957. He joined United as an apprentice straight from school in 1972 and turned professional two years later. He made his début that same season, coming on as a substitute for Martin Buchan in a 1–0 victory at Southampton. With his speed, strength and athleticism he succeeded Alex Forsyth as United's regular full-back. He was an ever-present in United's title challenge in 1979–80 when they finished second, their highest finish since 1968. He also won an FA Cup medal in 1977.

Ron Atkinson's arrival as United manager would inevitably create casualties and Nicholl was one of them. In 1981 John Gidman was signed from Everton in a swap deal that took Mickey Thomas to Goodison Park. Nicholl was loaned out to Sunderland before returning to Canada to play with Toronto Blizzards. He subsequently had a second spell with Sunderland before joining Glasgow Rangers and West Brom. He went on to become a successful player-manager in Scotland with Raith Rovers and succeeded Mick McCarthy at Millwall when McCarthy was made manager of the Irish international side.

Nicholl was capped 73 times for Northern Ireland, culminating in appearances at the World Cup finals in 1982 and 1986. Northern Ireland are not as famous for their generous application of the parentage laws as their southern counterparts. In 1980 Everton manager Gordon Lee rang up Billy Bingham to recommend one of his midfielders, Eamon O'Keefe, for the Irish squad. Lee was shocked to discover that he did not qualify because he was not Irish and indignantly asked, 'Well, what business has anyone got naming him Eamon O'Keefe if he isn't Irish?' Bingham replied, 'Probably the same business they have naming you Lee when you're not Chinese!'

George Best tells a wonderful story about Nicholl's involvement with the Irish team. In 1978 the Northern Ireland squad were making their way from their hotel to Windsor Park for a fixture against Iceland. Their manager was Billy Bingham, a very erudite man. Throughout the bus journey Bingham was enthralled by the book he was reading and oblivious to everything that was going on around him. Eventually some officials summoned him to the top of the bus, and George rushed up to see what he was reading. Nicholl asked him the title of this book. 'The Diaries of James Joyce 1930 to 1935,' George replied. A few minutes later Nicholl tapped Best on the shoulder and said, 'This Joyce must have been some kid. He kept a diary up to when he was a five-year-old child!'

Chapter Seven

Paradise Regained

Interviewer: 'How's the leg, Kevin?'
Kevin Moran: 'It's fuc . . . It's very sore.'

When Matt Busby died in January 1994 aged 84, the football world was united in grief. As a manager and, first and foremost, as a man he was peerless. For both reasons he was, in the words of Denis Law, 'the greatest ambassador the game had ever known'. By the time of his death Manchester United had become a very different club from the one he had built. In fact, it was no longer simply a club. It was a business.

Jeremy Novick captures the flavour of this change wonderfully. His *In a League of Their Own: The Maverick Managers* (Mainstream) sees the turning point as the start of the Ferguson era, when 'United turned from being classic aristocrats to being grubby money'. He sees the contrast between the playing styles of Bobby Charlton and Paul Ince as the epitome of the divided worlds of beauty and the beast. In his view, Paradise was lost to the god Mammon as United traded its soul for merchandising supremacy.

Kevin Baldwin's entertaining manual for fans *This Supporting Life: How to Be a Real Football Fan* (which suggests that the way to get into Old Trafford for free is to join a parachute team) has an amusing spin on this crass commercialism. He suggests that the word 'UMBRO' that appears on the team kit stands for 'United's Massively Big Rip-Off'. He goes on to point to the fact that sponsors whose names are initials are usually tailor-made for a club. Witness:

JVC (Arsenal): Just Very Cautious

LBC (Wimbledon): Long Ball Creed

NEC (Everton): Not Even Close

United became a public limited company quoted on the stock exchange in 1991. Eamon Dunphy is saddened by this. 'Manchester United are now a corporation run by accountants. Its values are corporate values so it is no longer a sports club. It is a corporation. That's a dramatic change, and it's regrettable.'

From the fans' point of view the '80s will be remembered for some stylish football and cup wins but the '90s would usher in an era of unprecedented success – in which Irish players would play a pivotal role.

Striker

Born in Harmonstown in Dublin, Frank Stapleton made his league début for Arsenal in March 1975 in a 1–1 draw with Stoke City. By the end of the 1980–81 season he had notched up 75 league goals for the club and had earned himself the reputation of being one of the most prolific centre-forwards in England. His tally of cup goals was equally impressive, Stapleton scoring 14 goals in 27 matches between 1977 and 1980. It was an important factor in Arsenal's three-year cup run in that period when they reached FA Cup finals in consecutive seasons, losing 1–0 to Ipswich in 1978, beating Manchester United 3–2 in 1979 and losing 1–0 to Eastenders West Ham (courtesy of a rare Trevor Brooking headed goal) in 1980. He also played in the European Cup-Winners' Cup final against Valencia (which starred Argentina's hero of the 1978 World Cup winning side Mario Kempes) in 1980 when Arsenal lost on a penalty shoot-out which saw Kempes, Liam Brady and Graham Rix missing from the spot.

Stapleton was voted Arsenal's Player of the Year in both 1977 and 1980, so when he left Arsenal in the summer of 1981 the Highbury faithful were bitterly disappointed – particularly as it followed so closely the departure of the fans' beloved Liam 'Chippy' Brady. Brady joined Italian giants Juventus for £600,000 despite the fact that Manchester United were prepared to shatter the British transfer-fee record with a £1.5 million offer. The fans' agitation was compounded by their belief that the club did not do all in their power to keep their two star players. However, in the cases of both Irish internationals their contracts were up and they felt it was the opportune time to seek a new challenge.

When the news of Stapleton's desire to leave Arsenal broke, the rush for his signature was immediate. Offers came from Italy and West Germany and the Irishman entered substantial negotiations with Liverpool. Stapleton was in Ireland for the second ceremony of his wedding and didn't want any disturbances, but when Ron Atkinson made the call and said get back to Manchester immediately, Frank responded. The fact that his new wife was a Mancunian helped to persuade him to choose United over Liverpool. Atkinson was less successful in his effort to persuade fellow Irish international Mark Lawrenson to opt for Old Trafford rather than Anfield.

A major wrangle developed about the size of Stapleton's transfer fee. Arsenal valued him at £1.5 million, whereas United claimed he was only worth £750,000. As the two clubs could not agree, the matter was decided by the Football League Appeals Committee, which valued Stapleton at £900,000.

Ironically, they could have signed him for nothing. As a 16-year-old he went on trial to the club but it did not really work out, and while United demurred about signing him, Arsenal's Irish scout, Bill Darby, alerted his employers and Stapleton was on his way to Highbury.

There is a famous photo of a very young Liam Brady, Frank Stapleton, David O'Leary and another youngster on the way to make it big in Highbury. The fourth man was future Irish rugby international Johnny Murphy. In the annals of Irish sport, 'Iron Toe' Murphy is unquestionably one of its most colourful characters. 'Irreverent' is much too tame a word to describe his famous after-dinner speeches as captain of Leinster. He had a bus and hearse business and turned up for training one night in his hearse with a coffin inside. Some of the players found it disconcerting to be doing their press-ups beside a coffin and grumbled to Johnny. He is alleged to have just said, 'She's not going anywhere and doesn't mind waiting.'

Spiderman

Ashley Grimes joined United from Bohemians in March 1977 for a fee of £35,000, having first come to prominence with Stella Maris.

As a schoolboy he had had an unsuccessful trial at Old Trafford. Just before signing for United he had agreed terms with Dave Sexton and QPR, but Tommy Docherty stepped in at the last moment. In an unexpected twist of fate it was Sexton who quickly had responsibility for nurturing Ashley's career at United.

In his six years at Old Trafford Grimes clocked up over 100 first-team appearances in a variety of positions: midfield, both flanks and full-back. In certain quarters his career at United is remembered for the wrong reasons. He hit the headlines when he was sent off for allegedly striking a referee in a match against West Ham, the press having a field day with such puns as 'Grim Day for Ashley'. As a consequence he was charged with bringing the game into disrepute and fined £750. Most United fans, though, remember him affectionately as 'Spiderman', courtesy of his long-striding style. His pace, intelligence and in particular his 'cultivated left foot' won him many admirers.

The 1982–83 season was very much a nearly one for Grimes. He deputised for the injured Arnold Muhren in the FA Cup semi-final against Arsenal and played a starring role. It seemed rough justice when he was dropped for the final against Brighton after the Dutch international had recovered from injury, especially as Steve Coppell was injured. Instead the inexperienced Alan Davies was selected. However, ten years later the myth that football is more important than life and death was painfully exposed when Davies was found dead in his car near his home in South Wales. He had committed suicide.

There was some surprise that Ron Atkinson chose not to give Grimes a run-out at Wembley in the replay of the final when he sat on the sub's bench and watched United win 4–0. His disappointment was intensified because he was United's first-choice penalty-taker at the time, and United got a penalty in the match which Muhren scored. United's other goals came from Norman Whiteside and Bryan Robson (two). United claimed their fifth FA Cup victory on Sir Matt Busby's 74th birthday.

In the close season Grimes moved to Coventry City. His finest hour, though, came in 1988 when he came on as a substitute to set up Brian Stein's winning goal in Luton's victory over Arsenal in the League Cup final. The following season he was back at Wembley in the final of the same competition but this time Luton lost to Nottingham Forest.

A Man for All Seasons

Dave Sexton's reign at Manchester United was celebrated in the song 'Onward Sexton Soldiers'. To no United player did the metaphor of a soldier apply more appropriately than Kevin Moran.

In 1976 Moran exploded on to the Irish sporting world with his spectacular displays for the Dublin Gaelic football team. Moran had played a few games for Bohemians in the League of Ireland in the 1974–75 season but as Gaelic football took precedence he dropped down to play non-league football with the UCD team, Peagasus. Ronnie Nolan, a coach at UCD, recommended Moran to Billy Behan. In 1978 Moran sensationally became a Manchester United player, for a nominal fee, having obtained a degree in business.

Moran was very different from the generations of Irish emigrants who had left for Manchester. In many ways he embodied the changing Ireland. In the early 1960s Ireland was typified by Eamon de Valera, a veteran of the 1916 rising who had survived only because he was born in New York and went on to become the dominant figure on the Irish political landscape for the next 50 years. His vision was of an insular Ireland of cosy homesteads, comely maidens and athletic youths. The '60s, though, were a decade of extraordinary change. The industrial revolution had bypassed Ireland but a new Taoiseach, Sean Lemass, wanted to drag Ireland, kicking and screaming into the modern age. Through an imaginative series of grants and tax incentives to foreign industrialists, he transformed Ireland from an agricultural and rural society with a predominantly old population resulting from the haemorrhage of emigration to a society that was industrial, urban and with a young population. The introduction of free secondary education took Ireland a further step on the road to a meritocracy.

A new era arrived in 1973 when Ireland joined the European Community. The bold decision to become enthusiastic partners in Europe signalled a move away from economic protectionism which had impeded Irish development since the 1930s, an abandonment of the notion that Ireland might flourish without involving itself in the EEC. The school curriculum reflected the multicultural environment. No longer would Irish identity be defined in terms of its separateness and difference from England. Moran typified the new, well-educated, self-confident Ireland.

Initially Dave Sexton deployed him in midfield in United's

reserves but when Ron Atkinson arrived on the scene he immediately moved him to centre-half, and in October 1981 he made his début against Wolves. Injuries to Gordon McQueen and Martin Buchan opened the door for Moran to win a place in the heart of United's defence.

Having won an FA Cup medal in 1983, in 1985 Moran became the first player to be sent off in an FA Cup final after being shown the red card by Peter Willis for a clumsy rather than malicious tackle on Peter Reid. A major controversy developed when Moran's medal was initially withheld.

A regular feature of United's matches throughout the '80s was Moran wearing a blood-stained jersey or head bandage, making scything tackles and attempting diving headers, immune to the threat to his own safety. He collected over 100 stitches, mostly facial, in his United career and gave enough blood to keep Dracula going for months.

An unforgettable photograph in *Edge of Madness: Sarajevo and Its City under Siege*, a book of photographs taken during the war in Bosnia, shows a young woman, immaculately attired, walking with immense dignity along a city pavement against a background of piles of sandbags and past a soldier who holds a machine gun. The caption reads, 'Looking proud and dignified, Meliha Vareshanovic's dress, demeanour and action are richly symbolic.' The writer of the caption went on to explain what her action meant to him. 'Her message to the surrounding Serbs is simple: you will never defeat us.' Moran's message to his opponents was loud and clear: 'Thou shalt not pass.'

Inevitably, given Moran's bravery, throwing his head and body where no sane person would, injuries came his way. Ron Atkinson once joked that he was going to give him a part-time contract because he never finished a match!

In 1988 Moran left United to join Sporting Gijon in Spain on a free transfer following over 280 appearances and 24 goals for the club. After a short stint in the sun Kevin returned to England and became a central plank in Blackburn Rovers' resurgence over the following four seasons. Although he was 24 when he won his first cap, against Switzerland, in 1980, he went on to win a total of 70. At 38 he was the oldest member of the Irish squad in the 1994 World Cup but injury robbed him of his chance to play any matches. During his time at Old Trafford, though, Moran formed an incredible partnership with another Irishman at the heart of the United defence.

Pauline Conversion

A porter peers out through the frost-covered window. Outside his colleague blows on his fingers. A bracing breeze blows through the bare brown trees. Two young girls play on the carpet of frozen earth. Nature seems whitewashed. Hands trembling with the cold, I walk into the Forte Crest hotel to meet the man with the most famous knees in Ireland.

An autograph-hunter competes for his attention. She is a petite, slim woman with curly red hair almost concealed by her woollen cap. Diplomatically Paul McGrath does the needful without eating into my time.

As I sit down he looks me steadfastly in the eye. His own eyes are soft and kind and so being stared at is not threatening for a stranger like myself. Yet he has a disconcerting habit of looking deep into your eyes and then into some unseen mystical place.

He speaks deliberately, thoughtfully, using his hands to help find and deliver the right words. His little asides are intimate, wry and chatty by turns. As we talk, two young children burst into the room unannounced to say hello to their hero. His eyes light up when he sees them. On moments like these when he feels totally relaxed he is much, much funnier than his grave, intense facial expression suggests. At times his customary shy smile gives way to a delightful grin. I have often since tried to put my finger on why this soft-spoken man made such a lasting impression on me, but I can't.

> Signing for United came as a great boost to me although I was never one of their biggest fans. As a boy I was a huge Chelsea fan going back to the time that they beat Leeds in the cup final replay in 1970 at Old Trafford. I never thought then that some years later I would be lining out for United myself. My hero as a boy was not George Best but Charlie Cooke.
>
> I played non-league football for Dalkey United. Their vice-president was Billy Behan, the great scout for Manchester United in Ireland. When I joined Dalkey, Billy's son Terry was in the side. It didn't do me any harm to be playing with Terry. Any player in that team who showed that they had the chance of making it in England was going to have a great chance of coming to United's attention. In fact Dalkey United were so keen for me to go to United that when scouts from Spurs came to see me play they whisked me away after the

match without really telling me why, and by the time the scout came into the dressing-room to talk to me I was long gone. Strangely enough I nearly joined Spurs after leaving United because Terry Venables, their manager at the time, was keen to sign me and I really admired him as a coach.

In fact Billy introduced me to the great Matt Busby. He no longer had anything to do with managing the club but it was a huge honour to meet him. What I remember most about him was that he was such a kind man. There'll never be another man like him at Old Trafford.

Terry Behan almost caused McGrath's career to take a slightly different route – a fact he recalls with wry amusement.

Ray Treacy was managing Drogheda at the time and my father introduced me to him. I was actually living beside him. I suggested to him that he should sign Paul and he came to see him play. Paul was playing centre-half. Normally we played him at right-full. When we were losing we put Paul up front and he scored two or three goals and then we pulled him back again to guard our lead.

When Ray came I couldn't believe how badly Paul played. I had never seen him play so terribly. I think Ray thought I knew nothing about football. All the same, he said to me, 'Well, listen, if you think he's that good I'll sign him.' I wanted Ray to make the decision for himself so I left it to him. Shortly after Charlie Walker stepped in for him.

My father had asked both Shamrock Rovers and Bohemians to sign Paul but they turned him down even though he was a friend of both managers. And even though he had recommended him to United, Dad was always worried about Paul in the early years. Paul was so easy-going and laid-back that my father wasn't sure if he had the temperament to go all the way. Dad went over to see him at Old Trafford because he wasn't setting the world alight at United. Paul said to him, 'Ah, sure, I can always go back to Pat's.'

McGrath quickly discovered that he had joined a virtual Irish enclave at Old Trafford.

I wasn't very long at the club till I found out that the Irish connection was so huge. There were a few young players from Northern Ireland such as the goalie Phil Hughes who went on to play for the North later on, Kenny Scott and, of course, Norman Whiteside.

It was something of a home from home for me with so many Republic of Ireland internationals at the club like Kevin Moran, Frank Stapleton, Ashley Grimes and, later, Liam O'Brien. There were also young hopefuls like myself such as Martin Russell and a young left-back from Dublin called Pat Kelch, who was a really skilful player but it didn't happen for him there and he came back to Dublin for my old club St Pat's.

Kelch was by no means an exception in failing to make the big breakthrough. McGrath readily acknowledges that there is a very fine line between success and failure for aspiring players at United.

Alan McLoughlin was one of the guys who looked like he had a big future at the club but they let him go. There were so many talented players then that a few were bound to slip through the net. I can remember David Platt being let go at United but he went on to make it huge with Aston Villa and England. Peter Beardsley joined United around the same time as me but only got one game with the club. I think back now to Billy Garton, who was a very promising centre-half but got injured and was forced to pack it in before his career ever got the chance to take off. When I think about it now I've been very lucky to last so long, especially because of my dodgy knees.

McGrath is at pains to point out that he is not the only player to make it against the odds. It is the experience of his good friend Norman Whiteside, though, that makes McGrath feel so fortunate about his extended career.

I met Norman as soon as I went to United on trial and we were in digs together. Although he was six years younger than me we hit it off straightaway. He might have been little more than a boy but he was built like a man and was a lot more confident than I was. In one of my first games for United's reserves, against Newcastle, I set up a goal for Norman.

Things went a bit sour for both of us after Alex Ferguson became manager. There was a lot about us in the press, especially about our drinking, and I crashed my car one night I was drunk. It was all bad publicity. Both of us were supposed to be heavy drinkers. I think someone called us the terrible twins of Manchester United. Ferguson had a go at both of us in his book. He never understood us the way that other managers I had like Ron Atkinson, Jack Charlton and Graham Taylor understood me. It was very clear to both of us that Ferguson wanted us out. Norman was a great player and it was a shame he had to leave the game at so young an age. He was a huge loss. Knowing what happened to him makes me realise how lucky I am.

In 1985–86 McGrath was runner-up to Gary Lineker in the PFA Player of the Year poll and to Gary Lineker and Chris Waddle for the Football Writers' Footballer of the Year in 1992 and 1993 respectively. With his bravery in the tackle, timing and keen football brain he made a big impression, although it took him two seasons to win a regular first-team place at Old Trafford. The high point of his United career came in the 1985 FA Cup final when he was voted man of the match as United, down to ten men, defeated Everton 1–0 after extra time.

When Alex Ferguson succeeded Ron Atkinson as United manager, McGrath's career entered more turbulent waters. Paul did not hit it off with his new boss and was fined £8,500 by the FA for criticising Ferguson. To add to his problems, his knees required eight operations, which kept him out of the side for long periods in the autumn of his United career. In his absence from the first team speculation mounted about a transfer with talk of a £1 million move to AC Milan. Liam Brady also tried to sign him for Celtic. Somewhat surprisingly, Ferguson and McGrath patched up their differences and in September 1988 the defender agreed a new contract. It proved to be only a suspension of hostilities, however, especially after a report from a top specialist which said that McGrath's knees would only hold up for a year. He was encouraged to quit football and take the insurance golden handshake but he declined and in 1989 moved to Villa Park.

It has been argued that selling Moran and McGrath represented Alex Ferguson's greatest mistakes. Eamon Dunphy has some sympathy for this argument but adds a qualification.

Alex Ferguson has done a magnificent job. It took him a long time to do it but I think he's been faithful to the Busby ideal of bringing in young players. He's been a magnificent manager and they've achieved a lot in defiance of critics like myself. He's stuck by this young team and a sort of hazardous journey with Eric Cantona and all of that. He has made mistakes, Cantona being one of them, but it was a mistake that served its purpose in terms of winning championships. Ferguson has been wonderful in terms of taking the long-term view and in the end is vindicated by his success with his young team.

A certain decision might *seem* wrong when taken in isolation and a particular decision may *be* wrong if it's taken in isolation, but for the historical judgement you have to see what he was really getting at and view it alongside the right decisions he has made. You can argue he was wrong to let Paul and Kevin go when he did but in the long run, taking an overview of things, he clearly had his reasons. His management has more often than not been vindicated by the decisions he has taken.

Wild Thing

Paul McGrath's great friend Norman Whiteside seemed to be the incarnation of the *Roy of the Rovers* fairytale. The cartoon character did not 'put himself about' as much as his Irish counterpart, though – on or off the field. With his strong, powerful frame he drew comparisons not so much with George Best as with the legendary Duncan Edwards.

In Spain in 1982, 'Stormin' Norman' became the youngest player ever to participate in the World Cup finals – taking that distinction from no less a player than Pele. The following year he became the youngest player to score in a Wembley final with a sweet strike on the turn against Liverpool in the Milk Cup and headed one of United's goals in their 4–0 victory over Brighton in the FA Cup final replay. He is perhaps best remembered, though, for his curling shot which beat Neville Southall for the only goal in the 1985 FA Cup final. By then Whiteside had dropped back to midfield where his lack of pace was less of a handicap and where his skill on the ball and aggression found a real outlet.

Following some highly publicised disputes with Alex Ferguson and a series of injuries, including Achilles and knee damage, Whiteside became unsettled at Old Trafford and sought a transfer. He missed most of the 1988–89 season with injuries and in the close season it was decided that a move would best serve the mutual interests of club and player. After more than 200 league games and 47 goals he was sold to Everton for £600,000. Sadly the Goodison fans never really got the chance to see him at his best and injury forced him to quit the game – though still only 25. He won 38 caps. After his retirement he went on to become a specialist in foot disorders and now supplements his income on the after-dinner-speech circuit.

From the Sublime to the Conspicuous

Post Office Social Club, Cormac Albion and Larne Town were Mal Donaghy's first clubs before David Pleat took him to Kenilworth Road for a snip at £20,000 in 1978. Donaghy had ten years of distinguished service at Luton before Alex Ferguson signed him for Manchester United for £750,000 – which was a big fee for a 31-year-old – where he formed an impressive central defensive partnership with Steve Bruce. He made over 100 appearances for the club before joining Chelsea for £150,000, a month before his 35th birthday in August 1992.

The only blemish on Donaghy's distinguished international record came of all nights in Valencia when Northern Ireland shocked the host nation, Spain, with a 1–0 victory to advance to the knockout stages of the 1982 World Cup courtesy of a Gerry Armstrong goal. Donaghy was sent off for the only time in his career. It was a harsh decision and slightly marred one of the most glorious chapters in Northern Ireland's history.

A player destined to become one of the great Northern Ireland wingers is Keith Gillespie. He signed for United in 1992 and made his début against Bury in the third round of the FA Cup a year later, scoring in the process. He played in United's Youth FA Cup final teams of 1992 and 1993 before leaving United, after fourteen appearances and two goals, for Newcastle in a shock £7 million deal which brought Andy Cole to Old Trafford. At the time Andrei Kanchelskis held firm control of the winger's position, but had Alex Ferguson been aware of the Ukrainian's disaffection and imminent plans for departure he would surely have been unwilling to let the Ulsterman depart. It is amusing, with the benefit of hindsight, to read Alex Ferguson's confident prediction in his 1995 book *A Year in the Life*: 'Andy will definitely get us 30 goals next season.' Fergie took Gillespie into the toilets to inform him about the deal before United beat Sheffield United 2–0 in the third round of the FA Cup on 9 January 1995.

Like every young pretender from Ulster with a bit of flair, the problem the youngster faced was that he was prematurely compared with George Best. Such comparisons are odious, as was implicitly recognised by the great Bill Shankly. He was once asked his opinion on the young Mick Channon. Shanks replied he was a very good winger. The reporter pushed him further and asked, 'Is he as good a player as Stanley Matthews?' The reply came: 'Oh, aye, he's as good a player as Stan – but you have to remember Stan is 65 now!'

Lurgan-born central defender Pat McGibbon joined United from Portadown in 1995-96. Given the competition for places, the Northern Ireland international served Swansea City and Wigan Athletic on loan in search of first-team football. Another young Northern Ireland international, Pat Mulryne, is also a promising member of United's squad.

One Night in November

Windsor Park on 17 November 1993 saw the battle of the two Irelands. The Northern Ireland team had a lot to prove. They had been subjected to chants of 'There's only one team in Ireland' the previous March in Dublin when they were humiliated in a 3–0 defeat. It was a decisive moment that could not fail to leave a legacy of bitterness. In the return fixture it would be a familiar battle cry: 'No surrender.'

Before the match Billy Bingham had turned up the temperature by labelling many of the southern Irish players as 'mercenaries'. There were bad vibes throughout. The words of the loyalist anthem *The Sash My Father Wore* were sung with fervour every few minutes and choice insults were bandied about with wanton abandon. Billy Bingham's celebration of the Northern Ireland goal was deemed by many observers to be a piece of unworthy taunting. Jack Charlton made a public apology for remarks he made to Bingham at the final whistle.

One player in particular was subject to constant taunting – former Northern Ireland schoolboy international Alan Kerneghan.

I grew up in Bangor in Co. Down and my parents still live there, but 'The Troubles' did not really impact on me. They certainly did on that night in Windsor Park. I've played in tense matches before but the atmosphere in the ground was the worst I've ever played in – it was hate, pure and simple. Things said beforehand made a bad situation worse. Billy Bingham's remarks really lit an explosive spark at a time when people were shooting each other as a matter of course. You just don't need that. Being constantly called a 'Fenian bastard' [although he was reared in the Protestant faith] is not too nice at the best of times but with my folks living there it was pretty uncomfortable.

Alan McLoughlin entered the annals of Ireland's top sporting heroes when his goal 12 minutes from time booked Ireland's passage to the World Cup finals in America. In the first half players from both sides sought to impose a pattern on the game but failed miserably. In the second half the tensions were even higher, but Jimmy Quinn worked a bit of magic to score a wonder goal. Then, soon after his appearance as a substitute, Alan McLoughlin found the net. Afterwards Jack Charlton remarked, 'That justifies his existence in the squad for the last two years.'

McLoughlin had signed for Manchester United as an 18-year-old in 1985 but 16 months later he was on his way to Swindon without playing for the first team. His career took a while to take off but once he came under the tutelage of Ossie Ardiles it rocketed. In December 1990 Ardiles was forced to part with his star midfielder, selling him to Southampton for £1 million, halving the club's debt at a stroke.

Earlier that summer his star ascended faster than he could ever have dreamed of when he became embroiled in one of the most controversial episodes in Irish soccer. At the last moment in the training camp in Malta Jack Charlton created a sensation by calling up McLoughlin and dropping Gary Waddock from the World Cup squad for Italy. The circumstances of Waddock's exclusion were terribly traumatic for him.

'Waddo' had emerged in the '80s as a tough-tackling and inspirational midfield general with both QPR and Ireland. Then things went horribly wrong for this genial and effervescent Cockney.

A knee injury in 1985 was the low point of my career. I

ruptured the ligaments in my knee and was forced to retire. I only ever wanted to be a professional footballer and it came as a hell of a blow to hear that the injury was so bad I had to turn my back on my dreams.

For every good player who has made a successful comeback, there are many more who have fallen flat on their face. The revival in Waddock's fortunes was neither swift nor painless. At the behest of QPR he agreed to settle with the insurance company and turn his back on football. It was obviously a shattering experience and one he is unwilling to discuss, at least on the record. Rehabilitation came via a sojourn in Belgium.

The way the insurance thing went I could only play amateur football in England or Second Division football in Scotland or abroad. I went out to Belgium and had a few trials. They went well and I was in the happy position of having a choice of clubs. In my two years in Belgium I never gave up hope that I could get back to the big time in English football. If you give up hope, what else is there for you? You've got to keep going and reaching for the stars. If you fail then at least you've given it your best shot.

A bizzare chain of events brought him right back to the upper echelons of the football world.

In 1989 I bumped into Jack Charlton at a dinner and he invited me over to join the Irish squad for a testimonial game. I played and it seemed to go well. Tony Cascarino spoke to the then manager at Millwall, John Docherty, about me, and I joined Millwall for two years. Shortly after, I was recalled to the Irish squad and played in a couple of friendly matches in the warm-up for the World Cup in Italy. When I had injured my knee my two aims were to get back into the First Division and then to play with Ireland. When I was called back into the Irish side I couldn't believe it, after being on the scrapheap.

Life could hardly have been sweeter for the born-again international as he flew off with the Irish squad for the World Cup and his date with soccer's élite. Little did he know that his world would quickly collapse on his shoulders.

> I can't describe how low I felt. One minute I was in the World Cup party and the next minute I was out of the squad and getting the plane home. I was devastated. Jack just pulled me aside and said I wasn't going to be included in the 22. It was as simple as that. He told me I could be the 23rd man but that was no good to me. As you can imagine it was very difficult for me, but I think it was even harder for Jack. Later I went to his room in the hotel and we had a chat. He explained why he was leaving me out but there was no consolation. I was sharing a room with Bernie Slaven at the time and he can tell you what sort of state I was in when I went back – but that's history.

Memories of that day still frustrate him. He was forced to watch the most glorious episode in Irish soccer from his sitting-room in his London home. However, he bears no grudges.

> I've met Jack since and we shook hands and had a chat. He had to name 22 players. That was his job and he did it remarkably well. His record is fantastic. My philosophy is to try and enjoy every moment while it lasts. Nobody knows better than me that it takes only one tackle and it can all be over. Jack did what he felt he had to do and that's why he was such a great manager, and I respect him for it. I don't think I could ever be a manager. I could be a coach but I don't think I could be a number one. There's too much pressure. There's only a certain number of people who can cope with that level of pressure and Jack is certainly one of them.

It is clear that Waddock has not allowed himself to be embittered because his career failed to deliver what it appeared to promise. He smiles genuinely and often.

> It is difficult at times. You have to keep motivating yourself. I've had a lot of highs. I'll never forget my first appearance for my country, or scoring for Ireland against Italy when they were world champions, or when we played Argentina and I marked Maradona. A lot of players don't have the highs I've achieved. Then again I've been unlucky with my injury and the World Cup, but I've got a smile on my face. I've played in the FA Cup final and represented my country and nobody

can take that away from me. When I am sitting there in my rocking chair when I am 70 or 80 I will remember those days.

Shamrock and Red

There had been a great deal of hype about Liam O'Brien's midfield performances throughout his League of Ireland career. Inevitably comparisons were made between him and Liam Brady. Cross-channel clubs were queuing up to sign him from Shamrock Rovers but a fee of £50,000 secured his signature for United. In addition United agreed to play the Hoops in two friendlies, in which the tall midfielder captained his new club against his old.

He made the worst possible full début with United – sent off after just 85 seconds against Southampton on 3 January 1987 – earning the dubious distinction of becoming the fastest sending-off in the First Division. Like so many before him O'Brien struggled to establish himself in the United side, although he was once described as 'the right-footed Muhren' because when he was in top form his passing was on a par with the Dutch master. He was denied the opportunity to get a settled run in the team – though most are, without consistently producing performances of the highest quality. He left Old Trafford in acrimonious circumstances, refusing a new contract and effectively walking out on the club. He joined Newcastle United for a fee of £275,000, and there and later at Tranmere Rovers he finally got the platform to show off his true talent.

The Ice Man

Denis Irwin became United's 50th Irish signing for a modest fee of £600,000. The Cork man had really made his name in Oldham's absorbing FA Cup semi-final saga with United in 1990. Born in the shadow of Cork's famous St Finbarr's GAA club, he attended Colaiste Chriost Ri and made a big impression in two areas: hurling and chess. He played at full-back for Cork Schools hurling team in Croke Park and his immediate opponent was his future international colleague Niall Quinn. He also represented Cork at the Community Games finals at chess.

His late father, Denis senior, had played for Albert Rovers, and father and son travelled together on the one bike to watch Cork Hibernians play. In 1982, much to the chagrin of his mother, Denis went on an apprenticeship to Leeds. There he stayed in digs with another future Irish international, John Sheridan. In January 1984 he made his Leeds début, and while he was a regular under Eddie Gray, Billy Bremner's arrival as manager saw him leaving the club to move to Oldham on a free transfer. On the same day in 1986, Terry Phelan was released. Eight years later the two men would be Ireland's full-backs in the World Cup finals against Italy. On the night the two looked more the part than the legendary Maldini.

Although initially earmarked for the right-back berth, the Irishman switched to left-back following United's signing of English international Paul Parker from QPR for £1.7 million. His contribution was immediate as United inherited the old Liverpool mantle of most successful club in the country. In his first season he won a European Cup-Winners' Cup medal after United defeated Barcelona 2–1 in the 1991 final. The same season he was in the United side which overcame Red Star Belgrade, the European Cup holders, 1–0 to win the European Super Cup.

The following season it was a case of third time lucky for Denis when he appeared in his third successive League Cup final. In 1990 he had been part of the Oldham side which had lost 1–0 to Nottingham Forest. The following year had seen him collecting his second loser's medal as United lost 1–0 to Sheffield Wednesday courtesy of a goal from his Republic of Ireland colleague John Sheridan. In 1992 he helped United to win the trophy for the first time in their history when they defeated Notts Forest, powered by Roy Keane, 1–0. Irwin collected his third loser's medal in 1994 in a 3–1 defeat at the hands of Aston Villa. To add insult to injury, Villa were managed by the man United sacked, Ron Atkinson.

In 1993 Irwin helped lead United to the promised land when they won the inaugural FA Premier League. Denis only missed two league games that season and apart from his sterling work in defence he contributed magnificently to the attack in his dual role as an attacking winger, supplying an unending service of dangerous crosses. He also notched up some spectacular goals, most notably a 30-yard scorcher against Coventry.

Irwin earned the nickname 'Mr Consistency' for his contribution to United's success. He has never dated any of the Spice Girls, nor Dani Behr, which is *de rigueur* for any footballer with pretensions to a star profile. The French sports newspaper *L'Equipe* did a feature on him under the headline 'His name is Nobody'.

Alex Ferguson once said of him, 'He comes into training, goes away and I don't get a word out of him. He turns out on Saturday and performs nine out of ten every time. You can always depend on Denis – and that's the kind of player you need to win champion-ships, the ones that give you eight and nine out of ten every week.' Those remarks capture the essence of Irwin – a man who does his talking with his feet. Fergie also stated, 'Defensively he's sound, he gets forward superbly to link play, he strikes a tremendous ball and he delivers crosses that forwards dream about. He's got the lot. He's been perhaps my best ever signing. He's been a sensation for the club.'

His temperament is such that he has been called 'the Ice Man'. If there was one incident which illustrates that, it was a Wednesday night in May 1995 as United and Blackburn were neck and neck in the title race. United were struggling to overcome Southampton. It was 1–1 with eight minutes to go, when a hotly disputed penalty went United's way. All the United players started to look around. Who would have the bottle to take the kick that might secure the championship? Irwin stepped up as the star names went absent. The fear of failure can chill the blood of the most hardened professional – witness hard man Stuart Pearce's missed penalty in the World Cup semi-final in 1990, not to mention Chris Waddle's orbit-chasing, botched effort. When it mattered most, however, Irwin showed nerves of steel and made no mistake ensuring a nail-biting *dénouement* on the final 'Super Sunday' of the season.

The Cork Mafia

Brian Carey almost made it a Cork mafia in Old Trafford in the 1990s along with Roy Keane and Denis Irwin. He began his footballing career with Albert Rovers before advancing to League of Ireland side Cork City. The formidable 6ft 3ins central defender was part of the Cork team which lost the 1989 FAI Cup final to Derry City, and within months he was bound for Old Trafford for a £100,000 fee – armed with a Diploma in Construction Economics.

In his four years Carey only made it to United's substitute bench and failed to make it into the side when United's regular centre-backs Steve Bruce and Gary Pallister were injured. Ironically, the high point of his time with United came when he went on loan to Fourth Division Wrexham, where he starred in the Welsh side's sensational victory over Arsenal in the 1992 FA Cup.

In 1993 his United contract expired and he was transferred to

First Division Leicester City. An independent tribunal set the fee at £250,000. Carey won three full caps for Ireland.

Roy of the Ramblers

In May 1993, when Steve Bruce placed the crown-shaped lid of the Premiership trophy on the head of Bryan Robson on one of Old Trafford's most memorable nights, it was a fitting coronation for Captain Marvel. However, not even Robson could go on forever. A replacement would have to be found for him – but it was a formidable task.

In July 1993 Alex Ferguson broke the British transfer record of £3.75 million for a 21-year-old Cork man when he signed Roy Keane from Nottingham Forest, after their relegation, despite some very stiff competition from Arsenal and Blackburn Rovers. As a teenager, Keane had written to most top English clubs asking for a trial but he hadn't bothered to write to United because he didn't think he was up to their lofty standards.

He was born and reared in a Corporation housing estate in Mayfield on the northside of Cork City, an area synonymous with Gaelic football. Keane took part in the national game in the corner-forward position. He also showed promise as a pugilist and never lost a fight in the boxing ring. Football writers would later go to town on his so-called 'rags to riches' story, even more dramatically claiming 'the boy from the ghetto done well'. Nice copy, but some distance from the reality.

He spent ten years with Rockmount FC, a well-known club in the northside of Cork. He had the good fortune to be part of a very successful side, with a number of his playing colleagues winning schoolboy caps for Ireland and drawing the discerning eyes of scouts from cross-channel clubs. Keane himself was not to the forefront of the scouts' attention. Following one trial game for the Irish Under-15 side, he was informed he was surplus to requirements because he was too small. It is difficult to match the diminutive, slight figure with the imposing frame which now fills the United jersey. It seems his body has been transformed.

When he was 17 he got a part-time contract with League of Ireland club Cobh Ramblers. Part of the package was a football course in Dublin. A year later he was signing for Nottingham Forest for a snip at £25,000. Brian Clough's comments would prove to be well founded: 'It's a long time since I've been so excited by a young man . . . I'd quite happily have paid £500,000 for him.' Less than a month later he was making his league début against Liverpool at Anfield. He was voted the Barclay's Young Eagle of the Year for 1991–92.

Cloughie said of his young protégé, 'I couldn't understand a word he was saying. But his feet told me all I wanted to know.' Soon came the accessories of fame, including a sponsored club car before he had taken driving lessons. To cap it all, Jack Charlton came calling and soon he was a regular in the Irish squad.

Every rose has its thorns, however, and Keane was to discover the downside of fame in the form of unwelcome attention from the tabloids. At times he played into their hands by swapping the sponsored car for a Mercedes with the number plate Roy 1. There was the story of an unsuccessful slander charge brought by a young woman. Then came a more high-profile 'incident' with former *Brookside* actress Anna Friel in which the Irishman was reported to have verbally abused her. Of course, there was also an 'altercation' outside a Manchester night-club. *The Sunday Mirror* made a big splash of a story of a messy flat he left behind him when he moved to Manchester under the emotive headline 'Roy's wreckage'. On the morning after Ireland's celebrated win over Italy in USA '94, *The News of the World* broke the story of a Nottingham lady who was having Keane's love child.

On 25 September 1997, in the early hours of the morning, he was caught up in a scuffle with two security guards, Dubliners Syd and David Pigott, in the Chester Court hotel in Stretford following a 2–2 draw with Chelsea. However, witness statements were withdrawn and no action was taken. In the match itself Keane gave a storming performance, prompting Alan Hansen to say of him on *Match of the Day*, 'Brilliant in attack, brilliant in defence and brilliant in midfield.' He was also interviewed by police over allegations that he threatened a neighbour during a row over Keane's straying dogs. Both incidents fuelled a tabloid frenzy.

His off-the-field antics were linked with his disciplinary problems on it. In 1995 he was sent off for the first time in his career for stamping on Crystal Palace's Gareth Southgate during an FA Cup semi-final replay. He was hit with a disrepute charge by the Football Association and was later fined £5,000. He was shown the red card twice in the first three months of the 1995–96 campaign, at Blackburn in August and at home to Middlesbrough in October. The following March he was sent off on his 30th appearance for the

Republic of Ireland against Russia in Mick McCarthy's first game as manager.

Even his father, Mossie, was embroiled in the tabloid frenzy and was quoted as having been a useful player who '. . . played some of my best games with five pints inside me'.

The comment did not in any way rupture the relationship between father and son. Keane's largesse to his family is widely acknowledged in Cork. Confirmation of this fact is that Mossie has acquired the nickname Sterling Moss. The Keanes now live in Rathpeacon, one of the city's most northern outposts. Keane retains a deep bond with his native city. As he grows older and travels, its delights have not diminished in his eyes, nor has comparison dimmed its many qualities. His umbilical cord is buried on Leeside, although trips home are slightly marred by those who turn a questioning eye on him. His working-class roots helped shape a personality that is independent and self-assured.

Irish sport has a tendency to get caught up in sideshows. The mind drifts back to Sonia O'Sullivan's defeat of the Portuguese world record-holder to win the 5,000 metres in the World Championships in Gothenburg in 1995. In the process she proved conclusively that she was the leading female middle-distance runner in the world. However, the ludicrous, whipped-up controversy about her alleged 'reluctance' to drape the tricolour around her cast an ugly shadow over her victory.

Like the Cork woman, Keane too has suffered from this tendency. In the summer of 1996 he went absent without leave as Ireland headed off on a summer tour to the United States. The affair was compounded by something of a PR disaster as he sought to build bridges with Irish manager Mick McCarthy which caused some Irish fans to boo him during a World Cup fixture and others to question publicly his commitment to the green jersey. Never before had this complex, sometimes tortured personality been so unfairly traduced.

The tabloids have not been as quick to pick up stories which show the other side of Keane. In 1994 he visited a young Bandon boy in a Cork hospital. The boy was suffering from a terminal cancer. Keane brought one of his football jerseys with him in addition to a football autographed by his Manchester United teammates. He spent a long time with the boy, and following his death the youngster was buried in Keane's shirt and carried the football in his coffin.

As the Irish team arrived home in Dublin Airport following USA '94, Keane noticed a young boy in a wheelchair who had travelled to welcome home the boys in green. Roy took one of his jerseys from his bag and handed it to the disabled boy.

Keane would probably appreciate the adaptation of the Genesis story. On the first day God created the sun; the devil countered and created sunburn. On the second day God created sex; the devil created marriage. On the third day God created a journalist. The devil deliberated throughout the fourth day and on the fifth day the devil created . . . another journalist. As a journalist and former player himself, Eamon Dunphy has a lot of sympathy for Keane.

> Roy has been dealt with very badly by all media. He has attracted a lot of criticism for his behaviour on the field and some of it has been deserved. Generally Roy Keane has been treated very badly, as are all people in the public eye, being misunderstood and abused by journalists in the interests of circulation. Roy is not alone but he's an easy target. To my mind he's not just an outstanding footballer, he's an outstanding man in the way he looks after his family. He's a decent guy. He has shown some of the excesses of youth but he's a great footballer and that's the only thing that matters.

A frequent theme in Alex Ferguson's recent books is the absolute centrality of Keane to United's current success. His pace, aggression, physical presence, passing, tackling prowess, aerial mastery, limitless stamina and incredible capacity for dominating from box to box make him a class apart – although his temper has periodically let him down. Keane has publicly stated, however, that without the destructive side to his performance on the pitch he would not be the player he is.

Despite all the plaudits he has not let fame go to his head and he has a nice line in self-deprecating humour: 'I just run around a lot.' Another asset is his versatility and he has successfully plugged a gap in emergency situations at right-back for United and as a central defender for Brian Clough. If anything his game improved as he revelled in the extra responsibility conferred on him in the United midfield following Paul Ince's departure to Italy.

In his first season he played an important role in helping United to become only the fourth team this century to win the double.

Another double beckoned the following season but the 'Eric Cantona incident' probably cost them further silverware. They finished second the following season and lost to Everton by the only goal of the game in the cup final. Normal service was resumed in 1995–96 as United became the first side in history to win a double double. Their fourth title in five seasons came in 1997.

For John Giles, Keane has been fortunate to be part of a team managed by Alex Ferguson.

> For years Matt Busby had been head and shoulders above any other manager in the history of English football but I think Alex Ferguson is now a serious contender for that honour. Busby was a pioneer. He was the first to build a side based on youth. It's incredible to think he won two league titles with a team with an average age of 22.
>
> Ferguson too has built a side based on youth, but he is operating in a much more complex environment than Matt Busby did. He is working in the era of Bosman, of free contracts and telephone-numbers deals. Sir Matt wasn't besieged by agents, nor did he have the top European clubs knocking on his door for key players every day. Players were tied into a system which meant that they had no option but to toe the line or face the football wilderness.
>
> The key to Alex's success is easy enough to spot. Football people know that the basic truth of the game is if you want to win, you need balance, pace and skill. You do not overload your players with fancy tactics. You just let them play. You also have to be obsessive, and Ferguson is as obsessive as anybody in football. Roy Keane and Denis Irwin are both lucky to have a manager like him.

If there was one match that encapsulates Keane's importance to United it must be the 1996 FA Cup final, when he nonchalantly nullified the threat of Liverpool's £12 million-rated Steve McManaman *et al* to ensure United's 1–0 triumph and be universally acclaimed as man of the match.

On 27 September 1997 Keane severed a cruciate ligament after an attempted tackle on the Leeds United player Alf Inge Haaland at Elland Road. Another indication of his import at Old Trafford was highlighted by Alex Ferguson's decision not to go public with news of the extent of his injury until after United had defeated Juventus

in the European Champions' League fixture. He admitted that
Keane was so important to the team that to announce the news
before the match would have caused a black cloud of doom to fall
on the club.

Chapter Eight

The Dream Team

*'All George Best and I have in common is that we were born in the
same area, discovered by the same scout and played for the same
club and country.'*

— NORMAN WHITESIDE

What is taken to the cup final every year but never used? The
correct answer is the ribbons for the losing team, but in the 1970s
one wag suggested Malcolm MacDonald following his dismal
performances for both Newcastle and Arsenal in that fixture.
'Supermac' was something of a folk hero to Newcastle fans, but his
inability to perform on the biggest stage cast serious doubts on his
claims to greatness.

What makes a great player? Is it natural talent or the ability to
inspire others? Alternatively, is greatness essentially a question of
spirit or one of attitude, a never-say-die mentality, an innate drive
to overcome all the odds, to put every ounce of energy to the glory
of the team? To what extent is greatness a matter of style? Does a
great player shape a football match in the same way as a great artist
uses paint on a canvas? Is physical presence a factor to be
considered? How long does a player have to maintain the highest
standards on the playing field to be considered 'great'? Can the
quietly effective player attain the same status as a gifted 'star'? Who
decides? And who decides who decides?

Greatness, like beauty, is an extremely subjective concept. It
could also be argued that to ask about the characteristics that make

a great player is to ask the wrong question. The proper question, since the different positions of a football team require such specialised skills, is what are the traits that make a player in a particular position great?

The problems of attempting the task of selecting Manchester United's dream team of Irish players are greatly magnified when one attempts the hazardous task of selecting the greatest players over different eras. In selecting my best XI I have to take into account not only the fact that in my opinion they might be number one person in that position on the field, but also that they would have the ability to gel with the other ten, so that in addition to the eleven best players I would get the best possible team.

From its inception Manchester United has had Irish players. Many of them have gone on to claim an illustrious part in the annals of the club. Others, like Tom Connell, who played just twice (1978–79) in the United defence, Derek Brazil, who made his début against Everton in 1989, Ballymena-born Tom Sloan, who had two seasons at Old Trafford, winning three caps for Northern Ireland (he made the starting line-up four times for United and had eight appearances as substitute), and Anto Whelan, who made just one appearance for the club as substitute, were less fortunate and never really made the grade at Old Trafford.

A temptation in selecting United's Irish dream team is to resort to the tactic of claiming any player with even a tangential connection with Ireland as one of our own. This would facilitate the selection of players like Pat Crerand of Irish Catholic stock. He joined United from Celtic in February in 1963.

Nobby Stiles, too, would be a contender – despite the fact that he was part of England's World Cup-winning side in 1966. His grandfather was an Irishman. A native of Wicklow, he left Ireland to find work on the railways and set up home in Collyhurst, a predominantly Catholic and Irish part of Manchester.

Furthermore, Nobby's brother-in-law is John Giles. In Giles's final season with United both he and Stiles were in and out of the side. Matt Busby had a habit of asking Nobby how he was playing. Invariably Stiles would say 'okay' and then Busby would inform him he was dropped. Giles advised his brother-in-law that he was handling the manager all wrong. When he was asked how he was playing he should always say he was playing brilliantly and that the team couldn't do without him. Stiles took this advice the next time the manager questioned him in this way. The only problem was that Busby asked an unexpected supplementary question: 'Yes, but can you play better?'

'Yes' was Nobby's instinctive reply.

'You're dropped for the next match,' was the boss's riposte.

In other company, though, Stiles was well able to get in the last word himself. Once, as Peter Hauser was writhing in agony after a tackle from Stiles, Hauser roared, 'The pain is excruciating.' Stiles replied, 'Excruciating? You can't be that badly hurt if you can think of a word like that!'

Jeepers Keepers

Unlike all other positions, Ireland has not provided the Reds with a rich assembly line of goalkeeping talent. However, seven Irishmen have acted as custodians of the United net: Billy Behan, Tommy Breen, Ignatius Feehan, Ronnie Briggs, Pat Dunne, Paddy Roche and Harry Gregg.

A hero for his role in rescuing people after the Munich crash, Harry Gregg would later show bravery in the 1966 European Cup quarter-final when United defeated Benfica 5–1 in the away leg. George Best had one of his finest games ever for United, scoring two goals. After the game, the Portuguese fans started shouting 'El Beatle' at him because his hairstyle was so similar to those of the Fab Four. One fan, however, charged at him waving a butcher's knife. Gregg rushed to his teammate's defence and wrestled the knife from his attacker. The police were quickly on hand and after interrogating the fan they discovered that all he'd wanted was a lock of Best's hair!

Gregg was hamstrung by a succession of shoulder injuries which cost him a number of first-team appearances and, frequently, caused horrific discomfort when he did play. There were times in the autumn of his career when he could barely lift his arm above his head, yet he persevered, displaying the same courage which had characterised his Munich ordeal.

Gregg remained with United until 1966, when David Gaskell took over from him in goal. From United he moved to Stoke before becoming a manager at Shrewsbury, Swansea and Crewe. His agility and dependability make him the number one on my dream team.

Captain Fantastic

There were four automatic selections in this fantasy side: George Best, Paul McGrath, Liam Whelan and Johnny Carey. The choice for captain is even easier: Johnny Carey has no credible opposition. Although Ireland has provided a surplus of talent at full-back for United, Carey has to be the first name on the teamsheet.

Carey was a very versatile star who lined out in no fewer than ten different positions for United – including emergency goalkeeper against Sunderland. Outside-left was the only position he did not play in for the Reds. In 1947 he earned the distinction of captaining the Rest of Europe against Great Britain at Hampden Park in the 'Match of the Century', and two years later he was voted Footballer of the Year by the sportswriters. In 1950 he was voted Sportsman of the Year.

Carey led United to a famous FA Cup final victory in 1948 against Blackpool, becoming the first Irishman to captain a cup-winning team, and the league championship in 1952. He was capped by both Northern Ireland (winning seven caps) and the Republic of Ireland (winning twenty-nine caps).

On his retirement this quiet, pipe-smoking man was invited to the boardroom as a gesture of appreciation for his magnificent contribution to United's success. Such was Carey's reputation as a man that he became known throughout the British Isles as 'Gentleman Johnny'. He died in August 1995.

A number of candidates present themselves for consideration as Carey's partner in the full-back position. Shay Brennan and Tony Dunne were the unsung heroes of the 1968 European Cup-winning side which prompted Matt Busby to describe them as 'regular as an army drum'. It was very difficult to ignore Dunne's claim for a place in the dream team and in fact the second full-back position provided by far the most agonising selection dilemma. The issue was decided for me following a chat with one of Irish sport's most charismatic personalities, and our favourite Englishman.

Saint Jack

The first thing you notice when you meet Jack Charlton for the first time is the speed with which he forgets your name. The conversation about football is peppered with comments like 'the boy with the great left foot' and 'that nippy little winger' which substitute for players' names. What is equally clear is that Jack has a razor-sharp brain and an encyclopaedic knowledge of the game. He talks affably about all the issues and personalities in football. Our conversation was not without incident.

The sun dipping into the horizon threw long streaks of bloodlike red into Jack's room in Dublin's Airport Hotel. In seeking his opinion on the Manchester United players who have played for him for Ireland, I had to compete with a nature programme or something to do with fishing on the television. As I got out my tape recorder he turned down the television to minimum volume and conducted the interview while keeping the corner of his eye on the screen. Occasionally he paused in mid-sentence when some arresting image caught his eye.

After an hour's conversation I was anxious to let him watch his programme in peace. I quickly collected my gear in Jack's cluttered room and bade him goodbye. To my absolute horror I discovered outside that I had departed with one of Jack's stockings. My first reaction was to run like the devil. How many people can say they have a souvenir of Jack Charlton's sock? Then I discovered the bitter truth of Hamlet's observation that 'conscience doth make cowards of us all' and I meekly returned with my tail between my legs. I was afraid that the former Irish manager would choke with laughter. Although I returned home sockless, at least I had the consolation of getting closer than any other journalist to the sole of Big Jack!

Listening to Jack talk, it is easy to feel overwhelmed by the sheer strength of his character. I wondered if he ever steps down from this heightened plane of existence to, as it were, the world of mere mortals. The question amused him without providing the series of revelations half hoped-for. He spoke of little without reference to the boys in green and to the importance he attached to bringing pleasure to the Irish football public. In Jack's distinctive Geordie brogue, most becomes 'moost' and goalkeeper becomes 'gullkeepah'.

His mind is as agile as an Olympic gymnast. When he talks about football he always seems, quite simply, to hit the right note. You can't ask any more of a manager than that. It doesn't bother him unduly that not everyone accepts his football creed. He does not expect all his critics to be converted to 'Jack Orthodoxy'.

A far cry from the hard man he is sometimes portrayed as, there are shafts of tenderness in all his comments. In conversation he is a star performer. When he is on his game, as he was then, there is none better. He thinks on his feet but, when necessary, kicks with his mouth. He is a complex character commanding respect and signalling friendship in the one moment. His eyes are shining, in spite of telling the story all over again for the umpteenth time, when queried about his glory days with Ireland.

I was afraid he would die laughing when I suggested that he would be canonised by the Irish people because of the success he has achieved with the team.

> Public attention is part of the job. I'm a miner's son from the North-East of England who has spent a life in football. They gave me a job to do over here which was to produce a team which would get results and bring people into the game. I've been very successful in doing exactly that. The fact that the people of Ireland like me is great. I like being popular. I would be a liar if I said I didn't. It's got its drawbacks. There is very little privacy any more. Canonisation? You couldn't have done that to me any way. I'm a Protestant!

Asked in particular about his opinion of Denis Irwin, the words come thick and fast.

> Denis is a wonderful player. I can't think of any time he ever let Ireland down. He was a big plus for us when he came into the side. He gave us extra options because he's a great crosser of the ball, a good tackler and he's great in dead-ball situations. He's a quiet lad who is dependability itself – if that's the right word. To be a successful football side you need different types of players. There are players like our Bobby who have that bit extra, who can see things that other players can't see and who make things happen for you and ensure you win big games. Sometimes they can be a bit annoying like Paul Gascoigne. They can be totally useless for 89 minutes and then turn the game with one stroke of genius. But no matter how many flair players you have, you need players like Denis Irwin who you know will always give you one hundred per cent.
>
> There are certain types of players who give managers headaches and I've come across a few in my time in the Ireland job. Denis, though, is a manager's dream, a class act,

a nice guy and a player you could always bank on to come up trumps.

Irwin just shades out Tony Dunne for the second full-back spot on the dream side. Selecting the two central defenders was a much easier proposition, even though there were some other candidates worthy of consideration.

Dual Star

If begrudgers were to choose a sporting subject for a screenplay they would surely choose Kevin Moran: a success in the academic world and in business and a man who reached the very top of the ladder in not just one but two sports. A sometimes-forgotten factor about Kevin is his goalscoring powers. He scored 21 goals in his 231 appearances for United and six for Ireland, the majority of them coming from set pieces when he attacked the ball powerfully to give the goalkeeper no chance.

Although he was not the tallest player in the world, he was very effective in the air because of his combative qualities. A revealing insight into his character comes from his mentor at UCD, Ronnie Nolan, himself capped ten times for Ireland.

> Kevin used to come to training at 6 p.m. and do a heavy training session with us. After a while he started to come to me about five or ten minutes before the end of the session to ask if it was okay for him to leave. I discovered later that he was hopping on his little motorbike and going to train with the Gaelic club in Drimnagh for 8 p.m. His commitment was amazing. He would turn out for us in matches and give his all, even if he was only half-fit because of injury. His dedication to his sport was awesome and everything he has achieved in the game and in life he richly deserves.

Moran was the rock on which so many attacks floundered and his courage and commitment earn him a deserved place in this fantasy team. His partner in its central defence is no stranger to him.

The Black Pearl

Paul McGrath's story is the stuff of movies. Born in Ealing, west London, in 1959, the future Black Pearl of Inchicore was brought to Monkstown, Dublin, where his mother placed him in an orphanage when he was only two months old. He lived in the main in residential care until he was 16. He left the orphanage at the age of 17 and struggled to adjust. In his teens he found his world dissolving beneath his feet and suffered two nervous breakdowns. He discovered the alternative Ireland, the socio-economic underworld where there are drugs, crime, unemployment and broken homes.

It is still difficult for him to talk about it. He is taciturn, even reticent. He averts his eyes from mine and gives the impression of one who is confounded to find himself the centre of attention. Although he has so many reasons for arrogance, he is the personification of modesty – the sort of man you instinctively want to protect. He speaks in a self-deprecatory and half-apologetic way.

> It was a funny time. I started to play for Dalkey United and things were going well on the pitch. We went on a tour of Germany. Things weren't so hot outside football, though. I was out in the real world for the first time and it was harder than I had expected. There was nobody there to pick up the pieces when I slipped up. I was not trained to fend for myself. It was not the best training for life.

He fights manfully to disguise his annoyance with any show of weakness. In deep despair and despondency, he was assured that to endure the present hardship was to enjoy later pleasures. He became one of the shining lights of those from humble origins, one of the very few men who had broken free of the usual constrictions and who had sought the rewarding adventures of the new life. He was about to break free from the rhymes, rhythms and riddles of his forebears and be transformed to greater heights thanks to the help of people like Frank Mullen and Tommy Cullen.

He came under the eye of Charlie Walker and was signed by Saint Patrick's Athletic. McGrath's unique talents as a soccer player persuaded United to part with £30,000 for his signature plus additional payments for first-team and international appearances. He was on his way to Old Trafford having secretly nursed an ambition to perform on the highest stage. The package also included a friendly between Pat's and United. Ron Atkinson described the deal as an 'absolute bargain'. Then came some of the happiest times of McGrath's life, memories of which have now dimmed the nightmare of those teenage years.

Success bred jealousy and the full glare of media intrusion. Mercifully McGrath is no paragon. There were times when he sought solace in the bottom of a bottle. This led to a lot of press speculation about his lifestyle. Apart from periodic binges, however, he never lost sight of his objectives. In the main he did not heed any rumours, he did not care for gossip; he was too busy tending his career and pursuing his ambitions to worry about what others thought. Although for years he was the undisputed star of the Irish soccer team and brought so much pleasure, he shines but he shines modestly.

In 1989 Graham Taylor brought him to Aston Villa for just £400,000 when injuries and problems related to alcohol had cast a cloud over his future. In fact McGrath's career flourished at Villa Park – although, amazingly, without the benefit of regular training. In 1992–93, as Villa pushed United relentlessly for the title, McGrath was voted the players' player of the year.

Having lost his place on the Aston Villa team at the beginning of the 1996–97 season, he moved to Derby County and helped them secure their Premiership status. In the summer of 1997 he moved to Sheffield United, but to the displeasure of most Irish soccer fans he was unable to make the Irish squad at the time.

In 1987 he played for the Football League in its centenary fixture against the Rest of the World. Against Maradona *et al* McGrath bestrode the élite of world football like a colossus. Most observers made him the man of the match. The performance spoke volumes about his genuine class.

Stormin' Norman

Midfield is probably the one area where Ireland has most consistently supplied United with a vast reservoir of talent, such as Tommy Jackson, Ashley Grimes, Liam O'Brien, Gerry Daly and Sammy McIlroy. McIlroy has a strong claim for inclusion in this dream side, but he loses out narrowly to one of his Northern Irish teammates.

By the age of ten Norman Whiteside had already made his mark as a footballer in Belfast, scoring 100 goals in the one season. In 1981 United beat off the scramble of clubs chasing his signature. The following year he made his league début coming on as a substitute for Mike Duxbury against Brighton and becoming the youngest Irish player to play for the Red Devils just two weeks short of his 17th birthday. His full début came in the final game of the season when he scored against Stoke in a 2–0 victory.

In his prime he was a fearsome tackler and had an exceptional talent for carrying the ball into the penalty area. He was also a great reader of the game and a wonderful opportunist, as was evident in his delightful lob over Ipswich goalie Paul Cooper in 1982. His eye for goal and his ability to produce the goods on the big occasion are the decisive factors which edge him into the fantasy team.

The Midfield General

John Giles was only 18 when he made his international début in November 1959. Ireland trailed Sweden 2–0 at Dalymount Park when the début boy launched a rocket of a shot to score a wonder goal. Two further goals from Ipswich Town's Dermot Curtis enabled Ireland to win 3–2. He is unquestionably one of Ireland's greatest ever players. Yet he poses a selection dilemma for the dream team: should he be included even though he played his best football after he left United? The fact is, though, he is simply too good a player to ignore. Moreover, his contribution to United could not be considered insignificant.

According to conventional wisdom the camera never lies. I wonder. My musings on this subject were prompted by my first meeting with Giles. Watching him on television I admired him as an intelligent, forthright and articulate analyst – far superior to some of his counterparts on ITV and BBC – but he seemed just a bit too serious. My first impression when meeting him in the foyer of the Montrose Hotel is that he is strikingly different from his TV persona. He is very warm, friendly, affable and good-humoured.

He goes in front of the cameras again in three hours to comment on a European Champions' League match. In his black suit, shirt and tie he is the picture of sartorial elegance. Is this by choice? He laughs and shakes his head: 'No. Some time ago we were asked if we could tidy ourselves up a bit before we faced the nation.'

Giles was born into a football family.

My father Dickie was a former League of Ireland player himself. He managed Shamrock Rovers at one point. He gave me a lot of advice but above all he gave me confidence in my own beliefs, which was a great help to me in my professional career because you can get a lot of bad advice.

He chooses his words carefully when asked what kind of man his father was.

He had his faults and his good points. Like most Dublin men he was a good drinker. He would be out a lot and was a very popular guy around town. He'd buy a few drinks for people. My mother should probably have got some of the money that he spent on the gargle. Like a lot of women in those days she had to struggle to make ends meet, to get shoes for us and so on. She knew hard times. When I went to England I was able to send her home a few pounds a week which made things more comfortable for her.

She too was a woman of her time. She never actually saw me play because she was too nervous that I would get injured. She always gave me a sacred heart badge to wear. Like a lot of working-class women she was very superstitious.

Giles has acquired superstitions of his own.

I always liked to see two magpies on the day of a match and, conversely, I always hated to see just the one. Sometimes you'd see just one magpie and you'd say 'Stop the car', hoping you'd see a second. Footballers are a very superstitious bunch. If they put on their socks one way and they play particularly well, you can be sure they will always put on their socks the same way after that.

During his tenure as manager Giles is credited with finally dragging the Republic of Ireland into the professional era. There were some occasions, though, when the amateurism of Irish officialdom got him down, as Ray Treacy recalls.

In 1978 we went out with a League of Ireland team to Argentina. It was, as usual, a real last-minute effort. We picked a team over the weekend and flew to London, where we stayed overnight. The next morning we flew to Buenos Aires via Lisbon and half a dozen other places. I think it was on the trip I decided to become a travel agent! We had a 28-hour journey before we got to Buenos Aires. We were shocked to see posters on the way to our hotel advertising a full-scale international between Argentina and Ireland. We got two or three hours' kip and then had a training session. After that we had a few more hours' kip before the match. Shay Brennan was in the party at the time and Giles said to him, 'I'd sign a contract now for a 5–0 defeat.' Shay said, 'I'll settle for 6–0.' Giles disagreed. 'No, that would be a hiding.'

We played in the Bocca Juniors Stadium. Some of our players had never been out of the country before and they couldn't believe the size of the stadium. It was probably Argentina's greatest team of all time and that was their final World Cup warm-up game. It really was a case of men versus boys. It was the most incredible result I've ever seen in all my playing days. We only lost 3–1.

I thank my mother for that. She is a very religious woman and she prays a lot to St Anthony. All her prayers for me must have been answered that night! A much fairer reflection of the game would have been 23–1. At one stage I really thought they were taking the mickey out of us when they started warming up this kid with long hair. I was convinced he was a ball boy. When he came on, though, the things he could do with the ball were amazing. It was Maradona.

After the game we took another 28-hour flight home after spending a day in Argentina and we were paid £25 for the trip. Anyone who thinks we were in the game for the money should have seen what we went through on that journey. I've many other stories like that about away trips with Ireland, I can tell you!

Treacy has great respect for his former Irish boss.

John Giles really changed things in Ireland and made things a lot more professional. However, he had one weakness. He couldn't say the words 'specific' or 'specifically'. Instead he said 'pacific' or 'pacifically'. When he gave his team talks he would always get it wrong and I would start pretending to row a boat, singing 'Row, row, row the boat, merrily down the stream'. It always made him red in the face and he would get really annoyed and bark at me to shut up.

To the astonishment of many people, in 1977 Giles turned his back on life as a player-manager with First Division West Bromwich Albion for League of Ireland football with Shamrock Rovers. It was a big cultural adjustment for him.

> My last game in England, the local derby against Aston Villa, was played in front of 52,000 at Villa Park. Then my next competitive game was in front of 92 in the Greyhound stadium against Thurles Town.

The Shamrock Rovers experiment, for all Giles's efforts, ended in disappointment. It coincided with another blow for him. Towards the end of his time with Ireland some of his fans turned against him – to the extent that he was booed whenever he touched the ball. He still can't fathom their hostility towards him and speaks with unaccustomed acrimony.

> I was surprised and hurt when I was booed. I didn't think I deserved that. I took over the Irish team when they weren't going very well. We never expected to qualify for any championship then but by the time I'd finished we did. I wanted to create an atmosphere in the side where we'd expect to win. I had a record number of moral victories playing with the Irish team, but very few actual victories. I wanted to get across to the players that we could get actual victories, and we got our fair share.
>
> When I was booed my reaction was, what's this about? I wasn't playing badly. By the end I wasn't booed. I think I won the crowd over just by my playing ability. Maybe I wasn't the average footballer or people thought I was too big for my boots. I never drank a pint in my life nor ever acknowledged the crowd enough. I was never very good on the PR side. I was worse than that, I was awful. I was always impatient with reporters because I constantly focused on the football end. I saw the PR thing as a nuisance.

As a player and a manager Giles had a similar reserved attitude towards the media as Kenny Dalglish. Once, after Blackburn had lost a crucial match, a journalist approached the Scotsman and asked, 'Kenny, can I have a quick word?' Dalglish replied, 'Velocity.'

Giles's ability to think of nothing but football often spilled over to family life, although there was one memorable occasion when he was brought back to earth with a bang.

> When I was manager of Shamrock Rovers I forgot that my wife was going to the clinic one day. We had four children then, the youngest was seven at the time, and that was going to be the end of it all. When I got home that evening I said nothing. My wife said, 'You never asked me how I got on at the clinic.' I replied, 'Oh how did you get on?' You could have knocked me over with a feather when she said, 'We're going to have twins!'

Giles, though, was not always so indifferent to his family's needs. He was for a time the regular penalty-taker at Leeds. When he missed one for the club his young son Michael was so upset that Giles refused to take a penalty for the club ever again.

Wired for Sound

But for the vagaries of the politics of Irish soccer it could have been Giles rather than Jack Charlton who led the Irish to the most glorious chapters of its history. What type of relationship does Giles have with Charlton?

> I met Jack first when I was with Manchester United. We were playing a few friendlies in Italy and Jack came along to see Bobby in the hotel. I was with Jack at Leeds for eleven years and I used to change beside him in the dressing-room, so I got to know him pretty well.

Was he surprised at Jack's appointment as manager of the Irish team?

> I think even Jack was surprised when he got the job. He was away fishing and had only expressed a passing interest. He didn't tout for the job, and didn't chase it.

The appointment provoked intense controversy at the time

because of Giles's treatment at the hands of the FAI.

> I've made a few mistakes in my career and that was one of the biggest I made, allowing my name to be put forward for the job. In the early stages I expressed no interest in the job and I think it boiled down to two people, Jack being one. It appeared that both were unacceptable to the FAI and I was contacted and led to believe I would get the job if I put my name forward – which I did – but I didn't have any great conviction in doing so. In fact, the only reason I did was that I was terrified of taking the easy way out and saying no. To be honest, when it was announced that Jack had got the job I felt a sense of relief. Now people can accept that or reject it. The idea that there were any sour grapes is completely untrue, although I think that was the general perception of the public. If people look at what I've done since and see that I've not tried to get back to management, they might get a clue to my plans.

He pauses and searches carefully for the right words when asked if he was treated shabbily.

> I'm being diplomatic now, but let's say it should have been handled a lot better than it was.

For Irish sports fans Giles is at least tangentially associated with the glory days of Irish soccer because of his role as RTE's soccer analyst. There he formed a popular and critically acclaimed partnership with another former Manchester United player, Eamon Dunphy – although their alliance generated no small amount of controversy.

Ireland went to the European Championships in 1988 with a reputation at least in certain quarters for playing a Wimbledon-type game. In this respect the only tactic they were allegedly capable of was the long ball. The Russian game gave lie to this perception as Ireland outplayed their opponents with the most stylish football they had played under Charlton's stewardship, culminating in a stunning goal from a Ronnie Whelan volley. The Irish were then denied an apparently blatant penalty in the second half when Tony Galvin was fouled in the box. Tragically, despite their superiority Ireland failed to book their place in the semi-finals when the

Russians equalised totally against the run of play on the counter-attack and with only six minutes to play.

In the post-match analysis, another chapter in what was becoming a familiar theme began when Giles and Dunphy once again drew attention to Mick McCarthy's inadequacies as centre-half. The 'McCarthy debate' raged throughout the country with some pundits passionately defending him and others equally vociferously claiming that Dave O'Leary should be in the team in his place. The debate inevitably seemed at times to be somewhat personalised, although Giles himself had no wish to engage in personal comments. He took a softer line on the issue than his co-panellist.

> I'm quieter about most issues than Eamon! He's very forceful but I was quieter than him, although I was saying much the same thing as him. I didn't think that Mick McCarthy was as good a player as Dave O'Leary. Mick's done exceptionally well for the Irish team when you look back at his contribution, but he was never in the same class as Dave O'Leary in particular. I would still feel the same thing today. Jack had a special liking for him and made him captain and you can't argue against his results.
>
> I can't speak for Eamon but I don't think I've ever made a personalised comment about football. I would hate to think I was criticising all the time because I don't think so. I watch football on ITV and BBC as a lot of people in this country do and there's nothing being said. People want you to analyse and give your honest opinion. I find now that over a period of time people accept you. If I now say somebody played well or played badly, people know I mean it. If I went on all the time and pandered to the public, people would soon see through me.

The RTE switchboard had been jammed following Ireland's victory over England with irate callers complaining in particular about John Giles's less than glowing endorsement of the Irish performance. Giles himself was a bit bemused by the controversy.

> People expected me to go mad with delight. I've never gone mad about anything. I tried to be as professional as possible. I saw my role to be one of an analyst and not one of a

supporter. Anyway, I'm not the type to go around with a green and white scarf around my neck and shout my head off, although I felt as deeply about Ireland's victory as anybody. I gave an honest view, but some people thought that I was sour because Jack had struck gold and I hadn't.

Jack's main appeal is that he is very successful. If Eoin Hand or I had achieved the same level of success, we would have been as popular. Success has a thousand fathers, as they say. Jack is quite rightly treated very well here and fully deserves the accolades he gets because he brought a lot of joy to people and brought them the success they craved for so long.

What about the famous 'incident' after the Egyptian game in the World Cup in 1990, when his co-panellist appeared to go a bit too far?

If Eamon had his time again he wouldn't have reacted exactly the way he did, but he was also misinterpreted. He was supposed to have said 'I'm ashamed to be Irish'. What he actually said was that he was ashamed of Irish football on the day and of the way we played. He reacted very strongly to it, which created a lot of controversy. In doing that he probably lost the message along the way, because all the talk was about his reaction rather than what he had actually said.

For all that, Giles clearly enjoys his role as analyst.

Analysis is not nearly as stressful as management. I haven't been shot yet!

He feels that his partnership with Eamon Dunphy worked because of the contrast in personalities. Their partnership and Bill O'Herlihy's chairmanship was memorably celebrated by the late, great Dermot Morgan in the much-lamented *Scrap Saturday* series when O'Herlihy broke the news that Dunphy was to have a child by Giles.

BO'H: 'Now, here to give the update on his life and love indeed is Eamon Dunphy. Sitting beside him is the proud Dad-to-be, John Giles. Eamon, how's your pregnancy?'

ED: 'Yes, Bill, this is a great pregnancy. I feel in a sense very maternal.'

BO'H: 'You're feeling presumably very paternal, John?'

ED: 'He is and I'll tell you something. Pregnancy is something that is great. Sperms have got guts and heart. They have the full DNA, chromosomes, the lot. Pregnancy is like professional football. Fertilisation is akin to winning a first - team place at Liverpool. Sperms are like professional footballers. They battle and they thrive, but the uterus is probably a hostile environment. The sperm that makes it through the egg, that is a great sperm.'

BO'H: 'You are mother-to-be and blooming and, if I may say so, you are showing a bit early . . . ha, ha, ha.'

JG: 'Great foetus, Bill, great foetus.'

ED: 'As John says, this is a great foetus . . . it's going to be another Gilesie.'

The Keane Edge

Joining Giles and Whiteside in the midfield of this fantasy team is Roy Keane. Keane had the awesome task of replacing Eric Cantona as Manchester United captain following the French star's shock decision to leave the club in the summer of 1997. That same year, on his video of his dream United team, Alex Ferguson described Keane as one of the best midfielders in the world.

His first season at United was not without its problems because of the burden of a record £3.75 million transfer fee and the inevitable comparisons with Bryan Robson, whose mantle he was destined to inherit. The young pretender in the shadow of the master. At Old Trafford Keane is called 'Damien' by the other players after the character in *The Omen*.

Jack Charlton gets very animated when asked his opinion of Keane.

He's not the greatest talker I ever met. There were times I wasn't really sure if he was listening to me, but when he really got going he was something special. He's got the most amazing engine I've ever seen. In the World Cup in America he put in a huge amount of work for us. The funny thing was that in that heat he never took any water during the match except at half-time. He could just run and run and run. He's a great battler and well able to put himself about. I know people say he's a bit hot-headed, but he never got into any trouble when I was in charge of him. I think people forget he's so young because he seems to have been around for a long time. He's the sort of player you would want to have with you rather than against you.

Disappointment is boldly stamped on Jack's face as he recalls one unhappy aspect of his association with Keane.

I know Alex Ferguson thinks the world of him and, to be honest, that caused me a few problems because he missed out on some vital games for us, especially in the qualification for the European Championships in England. Our squad is so small that we can't afford to miss out on key players in vital positions. Roy's absence left us very thin in the middle of the park for some vital games and we paid a high price for it. I know Alex pays Roy's wages, but maybe Roy could have played a few more big games for us. He is a very competitive lad and without him we weren't the force we could have been or should have been. But that's water under the bridge now. I'd like him to go on to even greater things for United and Ireland.

Whelan and Dealin'

If we were to apply the same criteria used to justify John Giles's selection on this fantasy team we would have to seriously entertain the claims of Don Givens for one of the forward positions. Giles's happiest day as manager of the Irish soccer team was that of the 3–0 victory over Russia in the European Championship qualifier in 1974. Apart from a hat-trick to Don Givens, the most noteworthy feature of the game was that it marked Liam Brady's début in the Irish jersey. Giles has great praise for his prodigy.

Liam was what we call a natural footballer – beautiful skills, well balanced. Give the ball to him in a tight area and he'd create something from it. He was a creator. As an 18-year-old in that Russian game, he strolled around the pitch as if he'd been there for years. Russia at the time were one of the best sides in Europe but Liam's maturity that day was phenomenal. He linked up with deadly effect with Don Givens – himself one of the best, if not the best striker ever to wear the Irish shirt.

Giles's admiration of Givens is shared by former Spurs manager Gerry Francis, who played with the Irish forward at Loftus Road. The erstwhile English captain is drinking his lunch – some kind of mineral tonic.

QPR had a great team in the mid-'70s. Liverpool only snatched the title from us by a point in the '75–'76 season. Practically all our team were internationals, from Phil Parkes in goal right up to Don at the front. We also had some wonderful characters in the side like Stan Bowles. It's only as I look back on it now that I realise how balanced we were and how much flair we had in the team. What we lacked that season was that our squad just wasn't as strong as Liverpool's and we had to pay a high price for that in the end.

Don Givens was an integral part of our success at the time. He got a lot of vital goals for us as he did for the Republic, although he was unlucky in the sense that he missed out on playing for them when they were going so well after Jack Charlton took over. He was a quality finisher with all the attributes of a top-class striker. I can tell you one thing: Mick McCarthy would be much happier drawing up his plans for the future if he had a striker like Don in his side.

Francis's admiration for Givens is shared by Ray Treacy, who played alongside Givens in that 3–0 victory over Russia. Treacy remembers that game vividly.

I've two main memories of that game: Don's hat-trick and the fear on their goalie's face. What caused that fear? I did!

Givens scored one goal for Manchester United in his nine appearances, four as substitute, during his short stay with the club.

He had joined them as a teenager in 1966. In 1970, at the age of 20, he was called into Matt Busby's office and told he was no longer required at Old Trafford – which was a devastating blow to the Irishman whose sole ambition was to play for United. He then moved to Luton for £15,000 before really establishing his reputation with QPR, where he scored 76 goals in 242 games. In 1974 Givens was given a rather unusual task. His teammate and fellow Irish international Terry Mancini was having such a run of scoring own goals that Givens was brought back to mark him every time QPR conceded a corner! He subsequently played for Birmingham City, Bournemouth, Sheffield United and Neuchatel Xamax in Switzerland. In 1997 he joined the coaching staff at Arsenal where he again linked up with Liam Brady. He won 56 caps for the Republic of Ireland.

Although Liam Whelan's career was cut tragically short by the Munich disaster which claimed his life, his legend will live forever. He was once hailed as the 'artist of the pre-Munich team'. Like Johnny Carey, Whelan was signed almost by default.

The similarities between Carey and Whelan are striking. Both were very unassuming men who were not in any way altered by fame or success. Both talents flowered in Ireland's most successful soccer nursery, Home Farm. The club's crest shows a man sowing seeds in a field and its philosophy is best summed up in the old Irish adage *Mol an oige agus tiocfaidh siad* ('Encourage the young and they will flourish'). Finally, both Carey and Whelan went on to become soccer legends at Old Trafford.

As a schoolboy playing for Home Farm, Whelan joined forces with former rugby international and Ireland's best-known entrepreneur, Tony O'Reilly. O'Reilly was a noted centre-forward who was good enough to get a schoolboy trial with Ireland once, but he did not turn up because of a rugby match. O'Reilly's enthusiasm for soccer may have waned on foot of an assault. During a match he made a bone-crunching tackle on an opponent, and the boy's mother rushed on to the pitch and attacked O'Reilly with her umbrella. The future Lions sensation remarked, 'Rugby is fair enough – you only have your opponent to deal with. Soccer you can keep, if it involves having to deal with your opponent and his mother!'

Tommy Taylor once said to Billy Behan, 'When we learn to think as quick as Billy Whelan, not a team in the world can touch us.' Bobby Charlton once wrote that he wanted to become the best footballer in England but felt he could never attain the lofty standards Whelan had achieved. At a football forum in Old Trafford in 1997, Noel Cantwell was asked about the great Duncan Edwards. The Cork man agreed he was a truly wonderful player but pointed out that he was once 'skint' by Liam Whelan when England played Ireland at Dalymount in a World Cup match.

Whelan was noted for his dribbling and as a master of the dummy and is perhaps best remembered for a goal he scored in the quarter-final of the European Cup in Bilbao in 1957 when he gathered the ball deep, weaved past five defenders and clinically finished. He ran with magnificent fluency and was graceful and elegant but also strong and menacing.

Few will quibble with his selection on the dream Irish side. The second forward to make this team is Frank Stapleton, for his ability in the air and his tireless, unselfish work as a target man.

To Be Frank About It

Stapleton became United's most expensive Irish acquisition in 1981, bought for a fee of £900,000 from Arsenal. Never one to be accused of understatement, Ron Atkinson declared that he had captured 'the best centre-forward in Europe'. Nobody, though, could disagree with Ron's assertion that he was a wonderful leader of the line because he was so aware of what was going on around him. He had the happy knack of being able to pull defenders out of position with his selfless running and set up great chances for teammates with delicate deflections and flicks.

The zenith of Stapleton's Arsenal career was scoring one of the goals in the Gunners' 3–2 triumph over Manchester United in the 1979 FA Cup final. When he scored for United in their 2–2 draw with recently relegated Brighton in 1983 (Ray Wilkins, with whom Stapleton forged an excellent understanding, also scoring a stunning goal for the Reds) he became the first player to score in the final for two different FA Cup-winning teams. United led 2–1 with only three minutes to go and Brighton seemed down and out when Gary Stevens equalised. Extra time brought a moment of high drama. There were only seconds remaining when Brighton got a gilt-edged opportunity to steal victory. Irish international Michael Robinson broke through the defence and set up a chance for Gordon Smith. The radio commentator said ' . . . and Smith must score . . .' but Gary Bailey saved his weak shot with his legs. The moment was immortalised in the title of the Brighton fanzine *And Smith Must Score*.

Stapleton made his international début against Turkey in October 1976 and marked his first cap with a goal. In May 1990 he scored his 20th international goal in Ireland's friendly warm-up for the World Cup against Malta, breaking his country's all-time goalscoring record set by former United player Don Givens in 1980. The summit of his international career was captaining Ireland in the 1988 European Championships.

After 286 appearances for Manchester United, including 21 as substitute, and 78 goals, in 1987 he was freed to join Amsterdam side Ajax. Sadly his stay there was not a happy one as he was dogged by back trouble. With the departure of manager Johan Cruyff to Barcelona, Stapleton found himself out of favour. He also played for French side Le Havre and Derby County, Blackburn Rovers, Aldershot and Huddersfield Town. In the 1991–92 season he became player-manager of Bradford City but was sacked in 1994 after failing narrowly to reach the Second Division promotion play-offs that year. His former Manchester United colleague Ray Wilkins brought him on to the backroom staff at QPR before he took up a coaching appointment in the United States.

Footballers Behaving Badly

Although George Best was one of a kind, he was a contemporary of players like Charlie George, Rodney Marsh, Stan Bowles, Tony Currie and Frank Worthington – players of genius who were precluded from fully achieving their talent because of temperamental deficiencies. Nonetheless, Best is a must for this or any dream team.

He was born on 22 May 1946. In the pre-Troubles era he grew up on the Cregagh estate in Belfast, where Catholics and Protestants lived side by side. As a boy he supported Wolves. He was an intelligent child, the only one in his class from Nettlefield Primary School who passed his 11-plus exam.

He is the most famous player to have played in the League of Ireland, making three appearances for Cork Celtic in the 1975–76 season. Best was football's first real pop star, with a consequent prurient obsession with his private life. Like Princess Diana he lived his life in a goldfish bowl and suffered the same aggressive intrusion into his privacy as she endured imprisoned in her media zoo. Few people would have emerged unscathed from that kind of hounding.

Like Alex Higgins he had the reputation of being a womaniser – a fact the Hurricane once acknowledged. 'I know I've got a reputation like George Best. I've found that it helps being world champion, especially at snooker. I always tell them [women] I'm a great potter. They know what I mean.'

Best's attraction for the opposite sex was brilliantly illustrated on a trip to the hospital following an injury during a match. A nurse brought him to a cubicle and told him to take off his clothes, saying that she would examine him in a minute. As he turned around to take off his clothes, Best asked where he would leave them. The nurse replied: 'On top of mine.' She had returned totally naked.

Best was the subject of a bewildering series of lurid storylines. There was an affair with Sinead Cusack, the most famous daughter of the Irish acting dynasty, who is now married to Oscar-winner Jeremy Irons. George had been dropped for missing training but travelled down to London to watch United play Chelsea. To avoid the media scrum waiting for him he detoured to Sinead's flat in Islington. Ironically his absence fuelled the circus even further and media and fans alike laid siege to Sinead's flat for the weekend. Even this incident provoked controversy, because Arthur Lewis, the MP for West Ham North, subsequently asked why it was necessary to waste public money providing Best with a police escort to take him far from the maddening crowd.

Then there was the time when Wilf McGuinness found him in bed with a married woman half an hour before United were due to leave for an FA Cup semi-final with Leeds. Leeds won 1–0 and Best had a stinker.

The most infamous episode of all was the Marjorie Wallace affair which almost coincided with his walkout from Manchester United. Ms Wallace was Miss World at the time and she had a two-night stand with Best which ended acrimoniously. Shortly afterwards he was arrested for allegedly stealing from her flat. After a short time in a prison cell, one of his friends mortgaged his house to have the soccer star released on bail. The case was dismissed and the judge took the unusual step of informing Best that he was leaving the court without a stain on his character.

Tragedy cast a more serious shadow on Best's life at the time when his cousin, Gary Reid, lost his life. Another in the long line of

SIMPLY RED AND GREEN

casualties of the Northern Troubles, he was caught in the crossfire while going out for a takeaway.

His battle with alcohol addiction, culminating in the débâcle on the Terry Wogan show, was not the stuff of good public relations. His wild friends Oliver Reed and Alex Higgins, though, rang him up and said, 'We don't know what all the fuss is about, George. You looked fine to us!' A United fan once said of him, 'If I come back in the next life I want to come back as George Best's fingertips.'

Without lapsing into clichés one of the traits which is often forgotten in assessments of Best is his wit. He once took the wind out of a reporter's sails by answering a prying question in the following way: 'If you want the secret of my success with women, then don't smoke, don't take drugs and don't be too particular!'

He also caught his United colleague Martin Buchan on the hop when he complimented Best on his new coat. 'From its style, it looks French,' he had said. Best replied, 'It is from France. It's Toulon and Toulouse!'

In the '60s Best was sometimes referred to as 'the fifth Beatle', given his popularity and status as a working-class hero. He was more of a Paul McCartney figure than a John Lennon. Every weird, well-intentioned step that Lennon took at the time – claiming that the Beatles were bigger than Jesus Christ, posing naked with Yoko, staying in bed to bring about world peace – was always ridiculed. Meanwhile, no matter what Paul McCartney did – taking LSD, getting busted for pot, discarding Jane Asher like a disposable napkin, being thrown into jail in Japan for possession of his favourite tipple – he was always forgiven.

However, as is the case with Lennon, no one can ever take away the memories of George's genius. Pele called him the greatest footballer in the world. He was, is and always will be simply the best.

My dream Red and Green team is as follows:

1. Harry Gregg

2. Johnny Carey (Capt) 5. Kevin Moran 6. Paul McGrath 3. Denis Irwin

4. Norman Whiteside   10. John Giles   8. Roy Keane

7. Liam Whelan   9. Frank Stapleton   11. George Best

Chapter Nine

Fan-tastic

'Ron Atkinson couldn't make it. His hairdresser died . . . in 1946.'
— TOMMY DOCHERTY

In the canon of sporting literature, surely the biggest irony is that the best writing on the beautiful game has come from – an Arsenal fan! Nick Hornby managed to achieve this feat in his classic *Fever Pitch*. He claims that 'the natural state of football is bitter disappointment, no matter what we score' and that football is a 'retardant'.

Apart from having the most popular fan base in Ireland, United also have the biggest anti-fan club! Popular broadcaster Des Cahill, according to a poll of radio listeners in 1995 Ireland's sexiest man, habitually wakes up the nation to slag off United on Ian Dempsey's popular radio breakfast show. He is the public face of a group which rejoices in the name of ABU – Anything But United. One United fan sought revenge on Des by recently describing his radio show, most unfairly, as, 'It is to nutcases what statues are to birdshit: a convenient platform upon which to deposit badly digested ideas.' Another listener claimed, 'Like skiing, it goes downhill fast.'

In fairness, it is United fans themselves who often dish out the harshest criticism of the team – witness the caption in fanzine *Red Attitude* under a photograph showing a plump, elderly nun kicking a football which read: 'David May models new team strip.'

RTE's balancing act to Des Cahill and strongest champion of

Manchester United is Ireland's favourite bird, builder, aspiring politician, pop star, television personality and national institution – Dustin the turkey. Dustin nailed his red-coloured feathers firmly to the mast when asked for a prediction of the clash between United and Liverpool: 'I think it will be a close match, so the score will be United 12, Liverpool 0!'

Frame and Fortune

Jason's snooker hall is the Holy Grail of Irish snooker because it spawned the career of Ranelagh's most favourite son, Ken Doherty – one of Ireland's best-known Manchester United fans. On a sunny Saturday lunch-time in September *Football Focus* is reviewing how Gary Pallister and Nathan Blake were both sent off on international football's 'fair play' day at the Reebok Stadium as United drew 0–0 with Bolton. A plethora of Ken wannabes are fine-tuning their skills. As soon as the world champion enters, everyone turns a questioning eye towards him. His opinions are avidly sought, his every remark hailed and his judgement accepted without question. The temptation to say that the young boy who receives his autograph is as happy as Jason returning triumphantly with the Golden Fleece is too great to be ignored.

Some enthusiastic young players forcefully seek his advice. Like all good teachers he is firm, forthright and clear-headed. But he is also extremely gentle with a soft streak of humanity, inspiring devotion among his 'pupils' because of his charm, humour and reasonableness. His genius as a teacher is that he is able to communicate and transmit his passion to his students and to awaken their creativity to take them on a magical journey of imaginative exploration.

With a week to go before the start of the new season Doherty is here for three to four hours' practice in the inner sanctum, which is a private room reserved for him with the table one of his sponsors has purchased for him. He is warm, affable and wonderfully articulate, yet there are glimpses of the determination, the obsessiveness and the single-minded ability to clear the mind of distraction, focus on the task in hand and almost put aside, sometimes for lengthy periods of time, the interests of family in pursuit of winning.

He is at pains, too, to reduce the romance and the drama of what his work is about, preferring to describe it in such prosaic and dull terms that he actually succeeds in conveying the sheer mind-numbing drudgery of much of his routine with unexpected vividness. Yet it is refreshing to see his passion for the games of snooker and soccer in a world where apathy is so prominent. A passion is all or it is nothing at all.

He jokes that he is delighted to be interviewed for this book.

Since I won the World Championship my mother has become more famous than me and it seems that all the requests for interviews are for her! She's a real Irish country woman. I think what clinched it for people in Ireland was the story that Dennis Taylor told on television during the final: that she had missed the match on the television because she got a puncture on her bicycle – when cycling to church to light candles and pray for me. [The religious ethos is confirmed by the first sight of the family home which rejoices in the name St Martin's.] Winning the world title has made an amazing difference to my life but for my family it has in some ways made an even bigger difference.

I don't know where I got my talent from. My grandfather played billiards but I didn't grow up in a sporting family. Even now my two brothers are not that interested in football. They might watch a match on television but they'd just as happily watch *Coronation Street* or *Eastenders*.

Growing up, I always wanted to be a soccer player. I played for Rathmines boys and at school, Westland Row CBS, I played Gaelic football, hurling and soccer. I played on the right side of midfield and sometimes as a central defender. Needless to say I wasn't the tallest centre-half in the world, but we had a very small team then!

As kids we were all interested in soccer. You had to be. You were either a Liverpool, Manchester United or Arsenal fan. We all collected stickers of the famous players and stuck them into our albums. My earliest memories of United were of the FA Cup finals in 1977 and 1979 but it was only as I got a bit older that I became a serious United fan. The thing that swung it for me was United's Irish connection. They've had so many great Irish players.

Frank Stapleton had a great temperament and was a great header of the ball [a header in the away draw with Dukla Prague in 1983 is cited as offering irrefutable evidence of this assertion], and he had tremendous dedication. Kevin Moran was such a brave player – almost too brave for his own good. What can I say about Paul McGrath? It's all been said before. He must go down as one of the all-time greats for both Manchester United and Ireland. Liam O'Brien was an exceptionally skilful player but he never really got a chance to establish himself at Old Trafford.

I don't think it is a coincidence that the most successful period in United's career came just after Denis Irwin arrived. I think Alex Ferguson described him as one of the best flank defenders in the world after United won the title in 1992–93 and no player was more consistent than Denis in United's double-winning sides in 1994 and 1996.

I attended the cup final in 1994 when United trounced Chelsea and the semi-final that year. It was great to see both Roy Keane and Denis play so well. Mind you, I was there the following year when Everton beat United, which wasn't nearly as nice! I've been lucky enough to meet Roy and Denis a few times when I've been at home for Irish games.

I think Roy Keane is now the heartbeat of Manchester United. He is such a consistent player and has amazing stamina. I love players like him who are fully committed and are workers. When he's ticking, the side is ticking – and he's usually ticking!

My favourite United player, though, was Mark Hughes. Sparky was twice players' player of the year [in 1989 and 1991] and although he had great power there was much more to his game than that. He scored some fabulous goals from incredible angles – often with his back to goal. I especially remember the cup semi-final against Oldham when Mark got a last-gasp equaliser with an incredible volley. Even by his standards that was a magic goal – probably one of his best [a narrow-angled drive in the Cup-Winners' Cup final against Barcelona and a memorable looping 25-yarder against old rivals Manchester City following the signing of Eric Cantona in 1992 as if in answer to those who speculated his United career was on the rocks are other worthy contenders for that distinction]. I firmly believe United sold him too soon [in the summer of 1995 to Chelsea for £1.5 million] because Andy Cole was not nearly as effective as him for a long time. In fact, I would still like to see him at United, where he could do a good job – perhaps from the bench. He always gave one hundred per cent and put his life on the line for the club, and that is the quality I admire most in a player.

That's why I was also a big fan of Bryan Robson. Robbo was a great battler – a real warrior – and Roy Keane has taken on that role so well now.

He laughs when I remind him of Barry Hearn's comment when asked if he was buying Manchester United: 'We're not into minority sports.' One former United player is a close confidant.

Eamon Dunphy is one of my best friends. Before I made it as a player he was a great help to me – finding out about grants and writing articles about me in the paper plugging me for sponsorship. When nobody in business wanted to know me Eamon was there for me and I'll always be grateful to him for that. He was there with me at the World Championship final. He's a real professional and in my view is the best journalist in Ireland. It's not just because he's controversial; he's a great writer and gets to the heart of an issue. His son was a snooker professional and Eamon is a wonderful writer about snooker. He always hits the target. Mind you, he once said to me, 'Ah, f**k, Ken, you're just too nice to be a winner.'

Winning the World Championship on 5 May 1997 was the summit of Doherty's career to date, but the icing on that cake came at Old Trafford.

After I won my world title I asked my agent to see if he could swing it for me to go to Old Trafford and walk on to the pitch with my trophy. I also told reporters that it was my greatest wish to do that, hoping it would improve my chances! Anyway, a few days later I got a lovely letter from Martin Edwards inviting me to come and parade at half-time for the final match of the season against West Ham. When John Parrott won his world title he wanted to parade his trophy in Goodison Park because he's a big Everton fan, but they had already played their last match of the season so he paraded at Anfield when Liverpool played Spurs.

On the day, I met Martin Edwards and he took me on a tour of the ground and brought me into the boardroom where I met Bobby Charlton, which was a big thrill. Then my big moment came when I walked on to the pitch in front of 55,000 people. It was like walking on to holy ground. After the match I met the players and it was nice because a lot of them are interested in snooker.

It was an experience I'll never forget and the perfect day in many ways. It was a real party atmosphere. United won 2-0 and had the Premiership trophy presented. None of us knew at the time but it was also Eric Cantona's last game for the club. The whole thing was a mindblowing experience and a real fairytale.

I have to say, though, that the one thing that topped Old Trafford was going out at half-time on Lansdowne Road during Ireland's 4-0 victory over Liechtenstein. That was the best ever. Every time I turned my head to a different part of the stadium I got a great reaction and a kind of Mexican wave began. It was like when Ireland scored a goal. I also got a great reception when I went to Croke Park for the Dublin–Meath match.

It was only when he established himself as a top-class snooker player that Ken began to frequent Old Trafford.

I was based in Essex and went to see United play in London whenever I could but I started going to home matches when Paul Ince got me tickets. Paul is a big snooker supporter and we met years ago when he was at the World Championships supporting Stephen Hendry. He heard I was a huge United fan, we got talking and the friendship began. He brought me into the players' bar a few times. I don't want to pretend we're best buddies or anything but we do ring each other and meet from time to time. I know people still remember his days as an angry young man when he always seemed to have a chip on his shoulder on the pitch, moaning at referees and snarling, but he's a hell of a nice guy. I think as he got older and since he got married and became a father he's mellowed and matured an awful lot. I was very disappointed when 'the Guv'nor' left United for Inter Milan because he was such a powerhouse for us in the midfield and almost the complete player. We still keep in touch. As a matter of fact, when I was winning my world title he was ringing his agent from Italy to see how I was doing during every frame. He rang me up afterwards to congratulate me. After he went to Anfield he rang me and said, 'I suppose you won't talk to me any more now that I play for Liverpool!'

I don't want this to sound like I'm only interested in United, though. I also follow the Irish team closely. I went to the World Cup in America, which was a great experience. I am good friends with Niall Quinn, who was at my world title win. I like to go racing with him and he's trying to get me more involved, although I am sitting on the fence at the moment. I do have an interest in one of his horses, Hoppin Higgins, which is named after Alex Higgins.

As a youngster my two heroes in life were Mohammed Ali and George Best. I have the videos of George's best matches for United and his finest goals. [The interview is temporarily suspended to allow for an in-depth analysis of Best's roasting of Chelsea full-back Ken Shellito at Stamford Bridge in 1964, his stunning display against Benfica, including two goals in the first twelve minutes, at the Stadium of Light in 1967, and a goal scored against Sheffield United during the autumn of his United career in the 1971–72 season which involved a spellbinding dribble.] He was such an outstanding player – in a class of his own. I don't think he had any flaw as a player, although obviously he had his problems as a person – but then again he had to handle an awful lot of attention and very few people could live like that. After I won the World Championship Joe Duffy did a radio programme about me and George rang in to congratulate me. I played him at snooker in town one evening. He wasn't half-bad!

A Lullaby for Tasmin

All seem soaked in a heavy despondency as if some totally melancholy spirit brooded over the place. Flies feast on the sea of slurry, and the buzz of their relish produces a faint hum in the air. It might have been the Sahara desert rather than a *basti* (slum) in Lahore. Poverty is sucking the vitality out of it as a bee sucks honey out of a flower. The *basti*, foul-smelling and decrepit, is a monument to broken hearts and foiled aspirations, to innumerable tales of sadness and dawning shreds of hope. It is easy to imagine that the stench would upset the stomach of a horse.

There are thousands like it throughout Pakistan, and every one tells the same story. Illness. Hunger. The death of hope. A person, it is held, can become accustomed to anything, but poverty for these people is a recurring nightmare. In the *basti*, as in most places, money, or more precisely the lack of it, makes all the difference. It is difficult not to succumb to a great sense of the desolation of life which sweeps all round like a tidal wave, drowning all in its blackness.

The Irish doctor is called urgently to a family home. The mother greets him warmly, like a long-lost friend. In the corner of the room lies a sick child, tossing to and fro in the bed. Tasmin is now in the full grip of fever. She is two weeks old, a pale little thing with black eyes set in a small face. Her face is drenched in sweat and the blue towel near her head is quite wet. The baby's little hands jerk convulsively outside the tiny blanket. She looks pathetically small in the bed, a tiny martyr in the grip of illness. Instinctively the mother is terribly afraid.

Suddenly Tasmin's eyes open wide and nothing has ever seemed so huge as those black jewels. They stare long at the doctor as if sensing his concern. Almost in spite of himself he looks deep down into their depths, and he knows that this child is suffering a great deal. The little, fragile hands open and close as if registering arrows of pain shooting through her frail body.

A few days earlier the cold of death had spread through every limb and bone in the baby's twin sister until she was very cold and stiff. It was only then that the torture had left her face and a soft peacefulness set on it like that of a child on a Christmas card. That night her mother's screams tore like knives into the heart of silence, ripping it relentlessly asunder. There was an animal-like quality to her wailing, powered by notes of horrifying, intense pain and desperation. Her screams fell like a sentence on the room.

As Dr Pat Ryan leaves that excuse for a 'house' three government jets, F-16s, costing a reputed 20 million dollars each, fly overhead, apparently on a military exercise. It is a real parable of the so-called Third World.

Back at his mobile clinic Dr Pat sips a foul-looking liquid. A few strands of grey hair announce his advancing age. He takes off his white coat and reveals his Manchester United jersey. Suddenly he is entangled in the clinging cobwebs of childhood.

I am one of the famous Irish diaspora. The candle that Mary Robinson had burning for seven years was for me! Like so many boys of my generation, I became a United fan when I was seven after they won the European Cup. I pestered my mother for six months after that to buy me my first pair of football boots so that I could become the next great Irish Manchester United star.

The only time I ever got to Old Trafford was a few years ago, to watch a game on New Year's Day 1992, the year United were battling with Leeds for the Division One title. Typical of my luck, United were thrashed by QPR.

The worst thing about Pakistan, apart from the poverty, the heat and the crazy driving, is that it takes two weeks for me to get videos of *Match of the Day*.

Strange as it may seem, my favourite United player was Ashley Grimes. He was an immensely skilful player who never got the credit he deserved. He was a very unlucky player. Every time he appeared to be on the verge of making it big with United he seemed to get an injury. He had a marvellous left foot and great stamina.

The Road Not Taken

Barry Kehoe has one of the most dramatic stories in the annals of Irish sport. At the age of 20 the soccer world seemed to be his oyster. Both Liverpool and Manchester United were fighting for his signature from Dundalk FC for a fee of £100,000. Few events have the power to send a tingle down the spine of soccer fans like a trial with the greatest club in the world. Barry had just played such a match for Manchester United's first team and had greatly impressed the United management.

> It was an unbelievable time for me. I had to pinch myself to believe it was really true. Here I was mixing with some of the most famous players in England and playing for the most famous club in the world. It was all a very big deal for a young fellah from Dundalk! I know this might sound insincere, but everybody at the club was very nice to me and encouraging. Nobody can ignore the history of the place and remain unaffected by the spirit of the past players. Here was I, so early in my career, playing for the club that was home to the likes of George Best, Bobby Charlton and Denis Law.

I had the good fortune to play a match for United. We played against Barnet and won 2-0, and I was lucky enough to play in the same midfield as Bryan Robson and Ray Wilkins. There were a few times during that game when I looked around and caught my breath because I was surrounded by so many household names. It was a real thrill for me and I remember thinking to myself, I could get used to this!

Barry modestly omits to mention that reports of the game were unanimous about the fact that he was man of the match, outshining his more illustrious midfield colleagues.

At the United training ground, the Cliff, ghosts of great players whisper from every corner. Every blade of grass has its unique memory of a great sporting conquest, but even as United's achievements were still fresh for the savouring, Ron Atkinson was speaking wistfully of his appetite for greater glory.

A glittering career at Old Trafford seemed inevitable for Kehoe. Then came the bombshell. Barry was diagnosed as having testicular cancer. Cancer is the most feared word in the English language. The memories of his trauma at hearing the news and of his deep psychological crisis will never be forgotten. 'When I heard the word "cancer", my mind went completely blank. I don't think I heard a single word the doctor said after that.'

Then came an emotional roller-coaster: his feeling of being invaded by an alien enemy; his dread of aggressive and unpleasant treatment; the fear of being in pain; the apprehension of becoming physically and emotionally useless; the trepidation of being a burden to his family; the uneasiness of losing his earning capacity and social standing. He experienced an initial sense of power-lessness because he felt he had no control over the disease or its treatment. No cancer patient is an island. It was also a hugely distressing time for all of his relatives.

I was brought up to believe that the doctor was second only to the Pope and that one didn't waste his valuable time asking stupid questions, and yet I wanted to know my 'enemy'. What could I and should I ask? Then there was the problem of telling family and friends: who do I tell first? How do I tell them? How would I react if they didn't respond as I anticipated? Was I becoming a cancer bore?

After chemotherapy and an operation in which he had one of his testicles removed, Kehoe started to pick up the pieces of his shattered career and boldly looked to the future with an intense determination to start afresh and begin to live a full life again. Following heroic efforts on his part he once again regained his status as one of the top players in the League of Ireland.

Six years after the initial diagnosis, Kehoe was discovered to have a murmur on his heart. He had open heart surgery and was discovered to have cancerous growths on the edge of his heart, which were surgically removed. Then he was discovered to have secondary cancerous growths which were malignant on his lungs, which necessitated further surgery and chemotherapy.

Eight years passed and Barry's personal and business life flourished, although he was never able to recapture fully the glory days of his soccer career. It seemed, though, that he had put cancer behind him. In October 1996, however, he became seriously ill again and further growths were discovered. Another cycle of chemotherapy began, and he now appears to be clear.

The winters have streaked past in a blur and Barry enjoys his life with his wife, Adrienne, and his six-year-old daughter, playing soccer with the local junior team and running 'Mr Ridleys', in Dundalk. Last year he extended his pub business to open a restaurant. Now 35, Barry lives under the threat of further revisits from cancer. He will never be able to speak of cancer in the past tense. Yet he continues to have a positive attitude.

> Initially I was very sceptical when my doctor told me that my attitude was crucial to my fight against cancer. I had a very fatalistic attitude to life, believing that outside forces shaped my destiny. Now I know that is not entirely true and that in many cases a positive attitude is the best ally a person can have in the battle against cancer.

Today the pride of Dundalk are the Corrs. In 1995, the hottest ticket in pop music, the family group of three sisters and one brother, released their début album *Forgiven Not Forgotten*, which quickly rocketed up the American charts. They followed it up with a worldwide smash *Talk on Corners*. Does Barry ever think he could have put Dundalk on the world map before them and does he feel bitter about what might have been?

I believe in living life in the here and now. It's only when people like you come along and ask me about it that I think about my brief time at United. Of course, it would have been lovely to have gone on and become a full-time professional with United and played in cup finals at Wembley and been a part of the great success Ireland had under Jack Charlton, but I can't afford to sit around moping and feeling sorry for myself. That's not going to feed my family.

In the Line of Duty: 13 September 1997

Since 1978 Irish soldiers have played a central role in the United Nations Interim Force in Lebanon (UNIFIL). Irishbatt, as the Irish Battalion is called, occupies territory in the south, some of which is controlled by Israel. Irishbatt is involved in the challenging and often hazardous task of maintaining peace and preserving stability. Two rival camps ensure the tension is ever-present.

The 81st Battalion is nicknamed GAABatt, given the prominence of the GAA connections on this trip. The Battalion Commander is former Roscommon footballing star Dermot Earley. Two of his deputies are Chris Moore, who trained Meath to win minor and Under-21 All-Irelands, and another former Roscommon star, Sean Kilbride.

For this battalion, a cloud hung over this trip when Clare soldier Private Gary Maloney lost his leg below the knee after a landmine exploded while a unit was in the process of making a roadway safe for use.

In the beginning was the word. Radio is the word. Radio is essentially blind. Its images are a private treaty between commentator and listener. The audience must fill out the game with description and information. The commentator dabs words on to an aural canvas.

The BBC World Service is featuring Manchester United's home tie with West Ham. The Irish soldiers who have a recreational break and the 81st Infantry Battalion are riveted. A poster on the wall states, 'Improve Morale. Increase Flogging.'

Most of the United players had been on international duty the previous Wednesday and for the first 20 minutes they looked sluggish. Both Roy Keane and Denis Irwin had starred in Ireland's 2–1 victory over Lithuania in Vilnius which effectively secured the Emerald Isle a play-off for a place in the 1998 World Cup.

Denis Irwin is left out for United's clash with high-riding West Ham, who are in third place in the table. All of the pre-match talk is of their rising star Rio Ferdinand. It is Roy Keane, though, who steals the show. After 14 minutes he whacks a rasping shot against the post. Almost immediately John Hartson puts the happy Hammers in front after a mix-up between Gary Pallister and Peter Schmeichel. United reply like a wounded animal and Keane sets up a glorious chance for Andy Cole, which is spurned. Within two minutes United are level. Keane again has a go from distance and the ball takes a wicked deflection off a West Ham defender and flies into the net.

In the second half John Hartson squares up to Roy Keane, but the Cork man doesn't react. As if to signal his new maturity, Keane even remonstrates with referee David Elleray when the striker is booked. Fourteen minutes from the end United get their winner when Paul Scholes heads a Gary Neville floated cross firmly inside the left-hand post. Panic ensues when Peter Schmeichel inexplicably drops a 40-yarder from Unsworth, only to scramble on it on the goal line. The Irish soldiers hanging on to every word breathe a sigh of relief.

Moments later the siren goes off in the camp. Shelling has started nearby. A calm voice booms out over the address system: 'Groundhog. Groundhog.' This is the cue for flight to the bunkers. The shelling is increasing. After a few minutes everyone is safely accounted for. As a calm descends among the Irish soldiers, a discussion on United's form gives way to a preview of tomorrow's historic All-Ireland hurling final between Tipperary and Clare.

Two hours later it is safe to return. The night is dark now. Black clouds hang in bunches in the sky and from time to time bright streaks of lightning run across the heavens.

Word comes from the communications centre that the Hizbullah have assassinated two Israeli soldiers, raising the number of murdered Israeli soldiers this year to 33. There is not a sound anywhere. Not a leaf stirs. Everywhere there is a calm, a stillness which speaks of peace, but a tense night is in prospect.

Theatre of Dreams

At the top of O'Connell Street a group of tuneless singers make up a raucous street choir, managing to turn the timeless classic 'Silent Night' into a contradiction in terms. The Christmas spirit is sadly lacking in the antics of the drivers in the rush-hour traffic.

Scurrying shoppers, arms laden with gift-wrapped Christmas presents, head home as the Dublin dusk descends. A little girl is mesmerised by Switzers' window with its glorious gnomes, who move majestically to the rhythm of the music. Crowds gather, young and old, just to savour the innocence of it all.

A sea of cards is on display, showing people in eighteenth- and nineteenth-century clothes walking about in snowy landscapes. A tree is decked out with stars and baubles, red and green and gold, crisscrossing in a kaleidoscopic display of colour. On the branches are little candles never to be lighted because of the fear of fire. On the top of the tree is a tin-foil star. There are little silver balls, lights like tiny stars and pale-coloured tinsel threaded among the branches. Near the top of the tree is strung a row of crinkled silver papier-mâché bells, each one with a clapper made from a varnished nut. Around the bottom are boxes of presents done up in pretty paper tied with red ribbon. This is a time of mystery, magic and, above all, children. Their excitement is transmitting like electricity, their shining faces a fitting reward to the idea of Santa.

The Ierne Ballroom in Parnell Square trades on fantasy on a Monday night as it is home to the weekly meeting of the Manchester United Supporters Club Ireland. From 6.30 p.m. a steady stream of callers come to book and collect tickets for United's forthcoming fixtures. Pilgrimage has taken on a new meaning as hundreds of Irish people regularly make the journey to England to see United play, home or away. The excitement is not directly related to the feverish preparations for Christmas going on outside, although the atmosphere is as Dickensian as Scrooge after the ghosts.

Two days previously United had beaten Liverpool 3–1 at Anfield in a match held in the morning to fit in with the demands of Sky Television's schedule. United went into the cauldron of old brimming with confidence, as befits a side with 31 goals in their previous eight league games. Andy Cole's two goals are verbally replayed and relived with relish, especially by the fans who had actually been amongst the 41,027 crowd. The first came in the 51st minute following a blunder from Bjorn Tore Kvarme and allowed born-again clinical finisher Cole to evade Matteo before shooting low into David James's right-hand corner. His second of the match, and 15th of the season, came from a side-foot from close in after Sheringham had nodded down a Giggs corner.

The superlatives, though, are reserved for David Beckham's goal from a curving 20-yard free kick which rocketed into a space in

James's goal that seemed to be no bigger than a mousehole. Even by his lofty standards the consensus is that it is one of the best free kicks in recent memory. There is amusement and bemusement that the tabloids make little mention of the wonder goal but go to town on the fact that he attended the Royal Variety Performance a few days previously with the mother of his girlfriend, Posh Spice.

The post-match comments are decoded with surgical precision. Alex Ferguson's remark is widely quoted: 'I think we're stronger than Liverpool. They are a young team, and that makes it more difficult when we play well like that.' The footballing deconstructionists claim that his exposition masterfully underlines the growing discrepancy between these two great northern clubs. Quiet satisfaction is taken from Sir Bobby Charlton's observation in the Anfield foyer: 'We're a good team.' It is all that needs to be said.

There is a real family feel to the gathering which is enhanced by the presence of a six-week-old baby. President of the club Dave Gregan jokes that he's a bit young to attend a Manchester United supporters' meeting. Mick O'Toole, the membership secretary, discusses the minutiae of the arrangements for the forthcoming Barnsley match. Here passion for the Reds is a genetic condition. Secretary Eddie Gibbons inherited his devotion for the club from his father and 'Manchester Unitedologist' Billy.

Over 30 per cent of the ticket-buyers are female. The club's most famous client is the uncrowned queen of Irish broadcasting, Marion Finucane, whose cousin is a member of the committee.

The supporters club was founded in Rosses Hotel Dun Laoghaire in 1969 in the wake of United's European Cup win. Its function was to organise support for Manchester United, and Sir Matt Busby was the main catalyst in its formation. He became the honorary president and has never been replaced.

A hundred people attended the first meeting. Today membership has increased to 1,700. The original committee included Frank Mullen, Noel Murray, Jimmy Ennis, Paddy Larkin and Des Healy. Initially the club organised six trips a season to United matches, but now it travels to every United game, home and away.

Originally it was known as South Dublin Manchester United Supporters Club, but in the 1980s it changed to its present name. The first task was to organise a dinner-dance, which went on to become an annual event. Guest speakers down the years have included Sir Matt (who came over with Lady Jean), Bill Foulkes, Tony Dunne, Shay Brennan, Tommy Docherty and Gerry Daly. The club also organises an anniversary Mass every year for the Busby Babes.

Above all, the supporters-club meeting is a place for nostalgia. The memories of great matches and star players linger for life in the minds of these United fans who grew up with them, leaving a warm afterglow to light up numerous conversations years later. These obsessive followers are *de facto* stakeholders in their performances, the intimacy of the relationship reflected in the thousands who have never even met the stars of United's past and present thinking of them as friends.

Older fans draw on the memories of decades ago. They remember their first acquaintance with the Busby Babes, when they knew intuitively that something special had arrived on the sporting scene, or recall the times they saw George Best glide through bedraggled defenders, making a feast from a famine of poor possession. The United stars appeal to the finer side of the imagination, with memory cherishing not only what they did but how they did it: with panache and elegance.

Hair Today, Gone Tomorrow

In their stories, songs, rituals, paintings, dances and, increasingly, in their writings, Aborigines continually recall the adventures of the sacred ancestors who created the world. The landscape is to the Aborigines the living cathedral which is the symbol of faith *par excellence*. It is there that the sacredness is experienced, and this is why the award-winning writer Bruce Chatwin speaks of Aborigines 'singing up the country', i.e. helping to bring it into continued existence. Accordingly, there is a continuous interaction between the past and the present, which allows Aborigines to think of their life collectively. Some Roscommon sports fans have the same facility, notably the town's barber and best-known Manchester United fan Paddy Joe Burke.

If every man is a king of his own castle then the court of King Paddy Joe has that indefinable quality called character. The greeting is hardly regal, although always warm and genuine. His shop is covered with pictures of Gaelic football teams. An essential element of the appeal of Gaelic games, that extra quality that distinguishes them from all other sports in Ireland, is the tribalism on which the structures are based. No other sports enjoy the intense rivalry that exists between clubs in the GAA. From time to time this creates problems, but in the main it generates a sense of community which has been all but lost in contemporary Irish society.

Paddy Joe wanders between two worlds. Born in the country, from the bowels of this land, he works in the town. His barber's shop acts as a unique bridge between rural and urban. Here, from time immemorial, pride in the honour of the parish is handsomely vindicated and vigorously defended. New influences are seeping into the lives of the locals in the guise of modernity as the bearer of the torch of enlightenment and as herald of the new age.

A haircut is one of the town's great social occasions. The weekend matches provoke intense discussion. Great sporting moments are dissected here with an insight and lyricism that Neville Cardus would have been proud of. Old controversies emerge from their caves of obscurity and are delicately excavated. The customers' talk is inevitably fascinating for many reasons, not least of which is that delightful blend of articulate bitchery and polite, well-dressed savagery. The comments represent, in condensed form, the spontaneous wit of the locals, charming little darts, wicked little stabs – though sometimes not so little – which are merciless, battering some poor unfortunate player, without relief or hesitation. Then conversation is abruptly halted when one of the fold's hairdo is completed and he is summoned to the world of real life. Many of the men go home the scenic route – via the pub.

One customer has a racing story. A punter in the Curragh bet £1,000 on the winner of the first race at 15/1. When he went to collect, the bookie told him he didn't have £15,000 in the bag. Could he drop back a few races later? He did, and the bookie, who was losing all round, still didn't have enough cash. Would he take a cheque? 'No, I bet cash and I want to be paid in cash,' he snapped. 'And if you're going to be running me around like this, I'd just as soon call the bet off!'

Then comes a blow-by-blow account of United's match two days previously when they stormed back from two goals down at Pride Park to snatch a point and boost morale ahead of a midweek Champions' League fixture against Dutch side Feyenoord. A few days earlier Alex Ferguson had put himself in line for an acting award when, after a much-depleted United side had been knocked out of the Coca-Cola Cup by Ipswich, he said earnestly and with a straight face, 'That's the best side I could have picked.' In front of Derby County's biggest crowd for 14 years, 30,012, goals from a Costa Rican and Italian double-act, Francesco Baiano and Paulo

Wanchope, had left the home fans in their new stadium singing, 'All teams who come here, there's nowhere to hide. Everyone is frightened of that Derby pride.'

United's plight would not have been so bleak had Teddy Sheringham not repeated his old Spurs party trick of missing a penalty. Derby's Estonian goalkeeper Mart Poom had felled Ryan Giggs as the Welsh wizard waltzed around him in the 29th minute. Sheringham's hard spot-kick was tipped around the post. Sheringham redeemed himself in the 51st minute when he rose magnificently to glance home a Gary Neville cross for his third goal in three starts. Six minutes from time Andy Cole drilled in his third goal of the season following relentless United pressure.

Outside, a traffic jam has struck the main streets and is spreading like the waters of a flood. Big cars belch forth thick, suffocating smoke – a proud witness to the progressive and modern spirit. It is a town of narrow streets, which is the cause of interminable traffic jams, particularly on wet Friday evenings. At its centre is the square which straddles two parts of town life – the market town, which brought farmers in from neighbouring hinterlands, and the industrial centre, which is slowly spawning new factories.

As everyone proudly says in those parts, 'Home is home.' This cryptic saying means that it is far better than all those places you could see on the television and that the blanket of green in which it wallows, sometimes uncomfortably, is to be preferred to the paved streets of the best cities of the world. Can anybody disagree with their logic? To dissent is to be disloyal to communal wisdom, and to be disloyal to that wisdom so carefully and painstakingly distilled through the ages is arrogance. And arrogance is the eighth deadly sin.

Paddy Joe is not just an armchair United fan. One incident epitomises his passion for the club.

> Since I first saw Man United win the European Cup in '68 there have been magnificent moments, but little did I know when the barber shop came to a halt just before three o'clock on FA Cup final day in 1985, when Man United beat Everton by a magnificent Norman Whiteside goal, that myself, George Bannon and a few friends were seeing history in the making. Peter Reid was in possession of the ball as Kevin Moran came in to tackle. It was a red card despite Reid's plea not to send Kevin off. Kevin was the first winning player to be refused a winner's medal when he went up the steps to collect it.

That action prompted the late Val McCrann, George Bannon and myself to send Kevin a medal on behalf of the Church Street Traders Association, Roscommon town. Kevin was delighted with our response and forwarded a letter of thanks back to the Church Street traders.

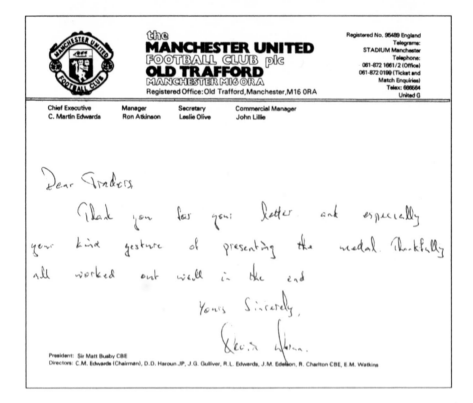

The Woman in Red

Death always sends a chill through the bones. Each death is a painful reminder of the ultimate and unwelcome end for us all. It is all the more harrowing when a young woman and mother is cut down in the prime of her life. Veronica Guerin's death, though, falls into a unique category.

Veronica was murdered by a contract killer as she sat in her car in Clondalkin on 26 June 1996. Irish society was shocked, as was evident in the unprecedented outpouring of grief and indignation that a young mother and celebrated journalist had been slain with such ruthless brutality.

The wall of flowers outside the national parliament, the minute's silence that was solemnly observed in workplaces throughout the State, the ocean of tears that flowed throughout the land and beyond as people tuned in to the television news footage of Veronica's funeral, especially the innocence of her son Cathal and the dignity of her husband Graham – these all touched the nation deeply.

The tie of marriage was not all that truly linked man and wife. They both had the same appreciation of the black humour of life, the same kindness and sensitivity and the same warm affection for friend and stranger alike. Now their love has become a burning spark in the flame of eternal love, free at last to love and be loved in an eternity that has already begun.

Veronica had shown heroic courage in exposing the evil that men do on the streets of Dublin. On a weekly basis she progressively stripped away the mask of anonymity that concealed criminal figures like 'The Monk', 'The Boxer', 'The Penguin', 'Warehouse John' and, most infamously, 'The General'. When her killer fired five shots into her body, it was the third attack on Veronica in less than two years, each one progressively more hideous. Death threats to herself and her husband and threats to the bodily integrity of her young son had been followed by the firing of shots through the window of her house. When this didn't gag her, a gunman was sent to shoot her in the leg.

The government responded to her death within days with a £50 million anti-crime package. It included many initiatives previously considered too expensive, including extra recruitment of gardai, more prison spaces and a Criminal Assets Bureau from which revenue officials, social welfare officers and gardai collaborate to deprive criminals of their ill-gotten gains. Even in death, Veronica continues to be a thorn in the side of the godfathers of Irish crime.

One of her biggest concerns was the way drugs were wrecking the lives of so many young people. Armed with the excruciating pain which knowledge confers on those who can discern the gulf that divides what is and what could be, Veronica knew these kids were acting out their lives against a backdrop of forces greater than they would ever understand.

She saw her job in vocational terms. In this vision the journalist must find herself supporting the widow and the orphan, the cause of the old age pensioner, the homeless, the poor and the outcast. She will question as to why some have an unacceptable standard of living. She will want to improve the quality of life for all those she tries to serve.

Speaking at her funeral, Fr Declan Doyle said of her, 'She dealt with matters that concern the life and death of our very society and our culture, the search for truth and sincerity and openness and tolerance, principles upon which a healthy society is built.' After her death she won several prestigious awards such as the person of the year and the American Narcotics Enforcement Association Medal of Valour. Veronica was the first civilian to be so honoured by the association. The most moving tribute to this extraordinary woman, though, was the tears from those who had never met her but felt they knew her as a friend – a poignant and appropriate homage to a woman who embodied the virtue of not counting the cost and who tragically paid the ultimate price.

It has been said: 'Be ashamed to die until you have won some victory for humanity.' When Veronica meets her maker on the ship of eternal life, bound for the shores of promise, she need not have any worries on that score.

In her too-short life Veronica was a regular visitor to Old Trafford. Long before it was fashionable or profitable she went absent without leave, on day trips on the boat to England as a teenager, to watch her favourite team. She was the irrefutable evidence of the untruth of Ron Atkinson's assertion that 'Women should be in the kitchen, the discotheque and the boutique, but not in football'.

Veronica was an Irish international in basketball, having starred for Killester Kittens. She also played soccer twice for Ireland and in that time she struck up a close friendship with her teammate Helena Stapleton, Frank's sister. Her passion for United was inherited from her late father, and as a girl Veronica's hero had been Denis Law. Whenever she played either soccer or basketball she always insisted on wearing the number ten shirt in deference to Denis. Her car always had to be red because of the United connection. Her love for football had a detrimental effect on her own love life, however – when she was dating her husband-to-be there was no question of going out on Saturday night because of the imperious need to watch *Match of the Day*.

Although Veronica's love affair with United stretched beyond two decades, one player had a special place in her heart – Eric Cantona. For her Cantona was more than a footballer. He added the intangible qualities of magic and mystique, which preserved the sense of continuity with the glories of United's hallowed past. Even when Eric transgressed the boundaries of acceptable behaviour, Veronica did not retreat behind the walls and pull up the drawbridge.

In normal circumstances the following aspiration would not be of great interest: 'Sharp are currently working on bringing 3D TV into your living-rooms. Mr Koshima hopes it will be so realistic that viewers will have to duck when Eric Cantona takes a shot.' However, what makes this press release from Manchester United's sponsors such a gem is that it was issued just before Cantona's flying kick at a Crystal Palace fan. As many sports fans bristled with moral indignation, Veronica stood by her man.

She was more interested in trying to decipher the meaning of Cantona's immortal comment, 'When the seagulls follow the trawler it is because they think sardines will be thrown into the sea.' No doubt this remark will be the subject of PhD theses in years to come in such disparate disciplines as philosophy, Anglo-French literature and sporting psychology. However, Veronica's favourite example of Cantona-speak came after the 1996 FA Cup final in which he scored the winner against Liverpool: 'I feel half-French, half-English, half-Irish.'

One of her most treasured possessions was a photo of her with Eric taken in the players' lounge after one of the games. Photos of that day, with other players, adorn the walls of their home, with pride of place given to Cantona's. Other clues of her love for United are the Ryan Giggs video under the television and the hundreds of programmes of old United matches that remain in the office. In this house Veronica is the silence, a voice that speaks without words, a quiet that is loud with conviction, the calm at the centre of a storm.

This home crosses boundaries where sadness and hope meet so dramatically. To walk in these corridors one cannot but try to listen to the secrets of a life lost. They have a music of their own, a melody of strange sadness and richness. The notes which enter one's consciousness are not, as might be expected, notes of loneliness, poignant cries of quiet despair, but notes of inspiration and encouragement. A dead woman's spirit lives again, somehow speaking to ears that belong to people not yet born – through the smiling face of her son Cathal. Nowhere are Emily Dickinson's observations more apparent.

> Hope is the thing with feathers
> that perches in the soul,
> And sings the tune without the words,
> And never stops at all.

Veronica's devotion to United was acknowledged by the club in the following letter from Alex Ferguson to Cathal.

The Manchester United Football Club plc

AF/LL

4 July 1996

Dear Cathal

I write on behalf of everyone here at Manchester United to say how saddened we were to hear about the tragic death of your dear Mummy, and our heart goes out to you and your Daddy. I know that you have been such a brave boy, your courage is something that will help your Daddy through the difficult days ahead, and I know that everyone is so proud of you.

Your Mummy was a very special and courageous lady, and you have shown those qualities, as young as you are. I hope that one day you can fulfil all the dreams and ambitions that I am sure your Mummy had for you, and grow into a fine young man with the same values that made your Mummy such a respected journalist in the eyes of the public and her colleagues.

We know that your Mummy was a big fan of our Club, and that you shared her love and passion for the game, and trust that you will have some lovely memories to treasure. We were all deeply touched when we heard that you had placed your United shirt with your Mummy, and we enclose herewith a new shirt together with some bits and pieces that we hope you will accept with our good wishes.

Your life has been struck by tragedy, and I know that words seem of little help, but trust that these words of comfort and the knowledge that you are in our thoughts and prayers, and those of the nation, will help to comfort you and your Daddy in sorrow.

Yours sincerely

Alex Ferguson C.B.E
Manager

Manager · Alex Ferguson CBE, Secretary · Kenneth R. Merrett
Telephone 0161 872 1661, 0161 930 1968 Ticket & Match Enquiries 0161 872 0199 Facsimile 0161 876 5502
The Manchester United Football Club plc, Sir Matt Busby Way, Old Trafford, Manchester, M16 0RA
Chairman & Chief Executive: C.M. Edwards, Directors: J.M. Edelson, Sir Bobby Charlton CBE, E.M. Watkins, R.L. Olive, R.P. Launders.
Registered office as above. Registered in England No. 95489. VAT No. 881 0985 31

Veronica had always dreamed that one day Cathal would tog out in the red kit of Manchester United at Old Trafford. On Saturday, 21 December 1996 the fantasy came true, much earlier than even she could have dreamed of. The icing on the cake was that it allowed Cathal to trot out alongside Veronica's footballing hero, the French poet and philosopher Eric Cantona. Cathal ran on to the pitch as mascot to the United side in the presence of the team's captain. Cathal provided the requisite lucky charm as United won 5–0, with Eric the Great scoring two goals.

Visual symbols and symbolic actions have a mysterious power and they reverberate in the memory: tearful, joyful citizens dismantling the Berlin wall block by block; a student kneeling in front of an advancing tank in Tiananmen Square; the red ribbons of AIDS concern and the white ribbons of peace worn in Ireland during the last IRA ceasefire; the broad smile on the face of Aung San Suu Kyi in 1996 as she emerged from six years of house arrest to meet the people of Burma with flowers in her hair; a million people in the streets of Spanish cities mourning the murder of a young politician by ETA.

Recent Irish history testifies to the power of symbols; witness the bowler hats and insignia of the loyalist Orange marchers. In many towns and villages in Northern Ireland the very stones of the street are painted in loyalist or nationalist colours. Huge murals, with their massive images of the 'armed struggle', lour over the street corners in towns on both sides of the sectarian divide. Most of the predominant symbols in Northern Ireland are sectarian: they stress difference, separateness, hostility and violence and, above all, they demonise the 'other side'.

Symbols define the community and its understanding of itself, its identity. Symbols give us our identity, our self-image, our way of explaining ourselves to ourselves and to others. Symbols determine the kind of history we tell and retell.

Veronica Guerin's coffin was draped in her Eric Cantona jersey. No symbol speaks more eloquently of the deep bond between Ireland and Manchester United.

Appendix 1: Billy Behan's Player Contract with Manchester United

An Agreement made the *Thirty first*

day of *August* 19*33* between *Walter*
Crickmer of *Old Trafford*
Manchester in the COUNTY OF *Lancashire*

Secretary of and acting pursuant to Resolution and Authority for and

ehalf of the *Manchester United* FOOTBALL CLUB,
Manchester (hereinafter referred to as the Club)

e one part and *William Behan*
1 Colley St. Stretford. Manchester

County of *Lancashire* Professional Football Player

nafter referred to as the Player) of the other part **Whereby** it is agreed

ows :—

The Player hereby agrees to play in an efficient manner and to the best
ability for the Club.

The Player shall attend the Club's ground or any other place decided
upon ~y the Club for the purposes of or in connection with his training as a Player
pursuant to the instructions of the Secretary, Manager, or Trainer of the Club, or
of such other person, or persons, as the Club may appoint. [This provision shall
not apply if the Player is engaged by the Club at a weekly wage of less than One
Pound, or at a wage per match.]

3. The Player shall do everything necessary to get and keep himself in the
best possible condition so as to render the most efficient service to the Club, and
will carry out all the training and other instructions of the Club through its
representative officials.

4. The Player shall observe and be subject to all the Rules, Regulations, and
Bye-laws of The Football Association. and any other Association. League, or
Combination of which the Club shall be a member. And this Agreement shall
be subject to any action which shall be taken by The Football Association under
their Rules for the suspension or termination of the Football Season, and if any
such suspension or termination shall be decided upon, the payment of wages shall
likewise be suspended or terminated, as the case may be.

5. The Player shall not engage in any business or live in any place which the
Directors (or Committee) of the Club may deem unsuitable.

6. If the Player shall prove palpably inefficient, or shall be guilty of serious misconduct or breach of the disciplinary Rules of the Club, the Club may, on giving 14 days' notice to the said Player, or the Club may on giving 28 days' notice to the said Player, on any reasonable grounds, terminate this Agreement and dispense with the services of the Player (without prejudice to the Club's right for transfer fees) in pursuance of the Rules of all such Associations, Leagues, and Combinations of which the Club may be a member. Such notice or notices shall be in writing, and shall specify the reason for the same being given, and shall also set forth the rights of appeal to which the Player is entitled under the Rules of The Football Association.

The Rights of Appeal are as follows :—

Any League or other Combination of Clubs may, subject to these Rules, make such regulations between their Clubs and Players as they may deem necessary. Where Leagues and Combinations are sanctioned direct by this Association an Appeals Committee shall be appointed by this Association. Where Leagues and Combinations are sanctioned by County Associations an Appeals Committee shall be appointed by the sanctioning County Associations. Where an agreement between a Club and a Player in any League or other Combination provides for the Club terminating by notice to the Player of the Agreement between the Club and Player on any reasonable ground the following practice shall prevail : A Player shall have the right to appeal to the Management Committee of his League or Combination and a further right of appeal to the Appeals Committee of that body. A Club on giving notice to a Player to terminate his Agreement must state in the notice the name of the League or Combination to which he may appeal, and must also at the same time give notice to the League or Combination of which the Club is a member. A copy of the notice sent to the Player must at the same time be forwarded to the Secretary of this Association. The Player shall have the right of Appeal to the League or Combination, but such appeal must be made within 7 days of the receipt of the Notice from the Club. The Notice terminating the Agreement must inform the Player the reasons or grounds for such Notice. If the Player proposes to appeal, he must do so within 7 days of the receipt of the Notice from the Club. The appeal shall be heard by the Management Committee within 10 days of the receipt of the Notice from the player. If either party is dissatisfied with the decision, there shall be a right of further appeal to the Appeals Committee of the League or Combination, but such appeal must be made within 7 days of the receipt of the intimation of the decision of the Management Committee, and must be heard by the Appeals Committee within 10 days of the receipt of the Notice of Appeal. The League or Combination shall report to this Association when the matter is finally determined, and the Agreement and Registration shall be cancelled by this Association where necessary. Agreements between Clubs and Players shall contain a clause showing the provision made for dealing with such disputes and for the cancelling of the Agreements and Registrations by this Association. Clubs not belonging to any League or Combination before referred to may, upon obtaining the approval of this Association make similar regulations. Such Regulations to provide for a right of appeal by either party to the County Association, or to this Association.

7. This Agreement and the terms and conditions thereof shall be as to its suspension and termination subject to the Rules of The Football Association and to any action which may be taken by the Council of The Football Association or any deputed Committee, and in any proceedings by the Player against the Club it shall be a sufficient and complete defence and answer by and on the part of the Club that such suspension or termination hereof is due to the action of The Football Association, or any Sub-Committee thereof to whom the power may be delegated.

8. In consideration of the observance by the said player of the terms, provisions and conditions of this Agreement, the said *Walter*

Crickmer on behalf of the Club hereby agrees that the said Club shall pay to the said Player the sum of £ *4 - 0 = 0* per week from *31st August 1933* to *27th September 1933*

and £ _____ per week from _____

to _____

9. This Agreement (subject to the Rules of The Football Association) shall cease and determine on *27th September 1933* _____ unless the same shall have been previously determined in accordance with the provisions hereinbefore set forth.

Fill in any other provisions required

If at any time during the period of this agreement the wages herein agreed to be paid shall be in excess of the wage by the Club to the player in accordance with the Rules of the Football League, the wages to be paid to the player shall be... amount the Club is entitled to pay by League Rules in force from time to time, and this agreement shall be read and construed as if it were varied accordingly.

As Witness the hands of the said parties the day and year first aforesaid.

Signed by the said *Walter*

Crickmer and *William Behan*

In the presence of *E. Connor*

(SIGNATURE) *E. Connor*

(OCCUPATION) *Clerk*

(ADDRESS) *77 Railway Rd*

(Sgd) *W. Crickmer*

(Sgd) *William Behan*

Appendix 2: Scott Duncan's Letter to Billy Behan about his Scouting Duties

Manchester United Football Club, Limited.

WINNERS OF THE LEAGUE CHAMPIONSHIP 1907-09, 1910-11.

Winners of Manchester Cup, 1908, 1910, 1912, 1913, 1920, 1924, 1926, 1931.   Winners of the Football Association Charity Shield, 1908, 1911.

WINNERS OF THE FOOTBALL ASSOCIATION CUP, 1909.

Winners of the Lancashire Cup, 1912, 1913, 1929. Joint Holders, 1920.   Winners of the Central League, 1912-13, 1920-21.

TELEGRAPHIC ADDRESS:
"STADIUM, MANCHESTER."

TELEPHONES:
TRAfford PARK 1661 & 1662.

SECRETARY · · W. CRICKMER.
MANAGER· · A. SCOTT DUNCAN.

OLD TRAFFORD,

MANCHESTER, 16.

Mr Billy Behan.
22, St Patrick's Villas,
Ringsend, DUBLIN.

17th Feb/36.

Dear Billy,

       I thank you for your letter of the 6th inst & regret I have been unable to reply to it sooner through being away in Scotland for the past week owing to the death of my Mother.   I only got back on Friday.

       I am very glad to note that the Free State football is improving & that a few very promising boys are coming along.

       Walter McMillen hasn't yet shewn me your letter with suggestions, so I must see him on Tuesday night when he comes down for training.   You know he is working now.

       I have read quite a lot about "GAUGHRAN" the Bohs centre forward. .   He will be an Amateur so if you know him, could you find out if he would like to come to Manchester.

       I could be doing with a good young goalkeeper, a big back, a good big inside or centre forward & an outside right.   Of course, any other outstanding player, I would be interested in too.

       If there is anyone particular that you would like me to see quickly, I can send over either Mr Bocca or Mr Broome, say on a Friday night & he could see a match on the Saturday & another one on the Sunday.   Let me know what you think.   Our team is playing very well at the moment & but for dropping a few silly points at home after having much the better of the play, would have been on top of League.   We should also have beaten STOKE CITY in the Cup,   They weren't in the game at Old Trafford & then the Referee beat us.

       The Reserves are also doing well—having won their last 6 games, including Wolverhampton, M/C City & Derby all away.

Now Billy, you can depend on me getting you two tickets for the Cup Final again this year, but at the moment I cannot say at what price.

We dont get our issue of tickets until the early April, so I shall keep you right, with two.

Messrs Crickmer & Rocca wish to be remembered to you.

You can do yourself some good by getting me a good player or two.

With Kindest Regards,

Yours Sincerely,

as Duncan

Appendix 3: Johnny Carey's Letter to Billy Behan

EVERTON FOOTBALL CLUB CO, LTD

MANAGER   J. J. CAREY

Telephone
AINTREE 5263

SECRETARY   W. DICKINSON

Telegrams
FOOTBALL LIVERPOOL

GROUND & REGISTERED OFFICE:
GOODISON PARK
LIVERPOOL · 4

OUR REF   YOUR REF   DATE

4th January 1961

Mr. W. Behan,
7 Durham Road,
Sandymount,
Dublin.

Dear Billy,

I was really pleased to get your letter just
before Christmas, and I hope that you will understand why it has
taken me so long to reply. Things have been fairly hectic here this
past few weeks, and although things are quieter now, I'm hoping that
we can stay in the Cup for a few rounds to maintain the great football
interest which is here on Merseyside. It is refreshing to have a letter
from someone who knows just what is involved in managing a football
club. Spending money as freely as we have done puts quite a strain
on the person mainly responsible. If I were buying machines, it I would
know what the machine would do, but when the articles are flesh and blood,
unpredictable, sometimes temperamental, it's a different story. I must
confess however, that we have done far better in the League than anyone
here had a right to expect, and I know that at least the Chairman realises
that fact. Others perhaps feel that because we spend a lot of money on
players, the right results should be automatic. So far, I have not
been able to field my strongest forward line; in fact, it may be not
until next month before they are all fit. In case you might be wondering
what I consider to be our best, it would be, Bingham, Collins , Young,
Vernon, and Lill.   But I have never known it to be so difficult to get
players !!!   Even struggling clubs seem to be able to resist the lure
of L.S.D. And of course, it is only in isolated cases where a player
becomes available who is gifted with ability, and has the temperament
to match. So many of them are the types that clubs are glad to be rid of.
I was with Matt last week at a do in Manchester
and I shall be seeing him again to-night, as we shall both be taking
our wives to the Irish Association Annual Dinner at Belle Vue. I know
that also with us will be the Irish Ambassador Mr. McCann who is
coming up from London.   But to get back to Matt and United. I'm very
pleased indeed to see how his lads are coming on. The very heavy grounds
will help players like Dawson and Foulkes, and possibly Setters. But
on paper at least, he looks to have quite a formidable formation, and
if he can add the added fire-power of David Herd, I hope we don't meet

EVERTON FOOTBALL CLUB CO. LTD

MANAGER J. J. CAREY   SECRETARY W. DICKINSON

Telephone   *Telegrams*

AINTREE 5263   FOOTBALL LIVERPOOL

GROUND & REGISTERED OFFICE
GOODISON PARK
LIVERPOOL · 4

OUR REF   YOUR REF   DATE

them before the Final. Matt seemed a lot better last week. He was very worried about his team, but this recent good spell will do more for him than all the doctors.

Now for a bit of home news. All the children are very well, and Patricia is now getting to the stage when she wants to make everybody laugh. She rolls her head from side to side, blinking her eyes, and when we show how funny we think it is, she does it all the more. Margaret is fine too, but we don't often get much chance of an evening out together as she does not like leaving the baby whilst she (the Baby) is so young. We don't fancy going to the pictures unless there is something really good on, so we usually settle for a meal at the Bold Hotel in Southport. It's funny how much wives appreciate having a meal out, but perhaps it's the thought that they don't have to wash up afterwards. I expect that Vera feels the same way.

I suppose you noticed that United and Everton Youth teams have won through the opposition in Lancashire, and we are now in the last sixteen, which is more of a regional draw. United home to Sunderland and Everton away to Middlesborough. We have arranged our matc for January 18th.

Well Billy I am expecting Derek Hodgson of the Daily Express here in a few minutes for some gen on our chances against Sheffield United in the Cup on Saturday, so I'll sign off, with my best respects to Vera, yourself and your family.

Yours sincerely,

Jack

June

| 18 | 19 | 20 | 21 |

[22 Sat] — [23] 24 25

26 27 28 [29]

[30] ~~31~~

July

1 M	2	3 wed	4	5
6 Sat	[7]	8	9	10
11	12	13 Sat	[14]	15
16	17	18	19	20 Sat
[21]	22	23	24	25
26	27 Sat	[28]	29	30 Tues